LIBYA

PROFILES • NATIONS OF THE CONTEMPORARY MIDDLE EAST
Bernard Reich and David E. Long, Series Editors

Libya: Qadhafi's Revolution and the Modern State, Lillian Craig Harris

Turkey: Coping with Crisis, George S. Harris

Israel: Land of Tradition and Conflict, Bernard Reich

The Republic of Lebanon: Nation in Jeopardy, David C. Gordon

Jordan: Crossroads of Middle Eastern Events, Peter Gubser

South Yemen: A Marxist Republic in Arabia, Robert W. Stookey

Syria: Modern State in an Ancient Land, John F. Devlin

The Sudan: Unity and Diversity in a Multicultural State, John Obert Voll and Sarah Potts Voll

Bahrain: The Modernization of Autocracy, Fred Lawson

The United Arab Emirates: A Venture in Unity, Malcolm C. Peck

North Yemen, Manfred W. Wenner

Iran: At War with History, John W. Limbert

Algeria: The Revolution Institutionalized, John P. Entelis

Afghanistan, Ralph H. Magnus

Oman, Calvin H. Allen, Jr.

Tunisia, Kenneth J. Perkins

ABOUT THE BOOK AND AUTHOR

This interpretive analysis of Libya provides a comprehensive look at the social, cultural, political, and economic forces that shape the country today. A concise history of Libya outlines the changes that have occurred in this Mediterranean/African state during the past several decades, emphasizing the period following the 1969 revolution. The determining and pervasive influence of Qadhafi as man and leader are examined in light of the origins of his ideas.

Dr. Harris devotes a major portion of the book to Libya's political system and to the structure of Libyan society under Qadhafi's Third Universal Theory. The power structures of the country—military, tribal, economic, religious—are treated in the context of continuity and rapid change, the two major social determinants of modern Libyan society and politics. The foreign policy of the Libyan Jamahiriyya is also examined in detail: Dr. Harris discusses Tripoli's major regional and global relations as well as Libya's role as an actor in major international disputes.

The discussion of Libya's economic resources, both potential and actual, gives particular attention to petroleum as the economic base of the country's political entity. Dr. Harris offers projections for Libya's post-petroleum economy and looks also at how the interplay of economic, political, and social forces may chart Libya's future.

Lillian Craig Harris has spent several years in the Arab world as a teacher, UN public information officer, and foreign service officer and has served as the political analyst for North Africa in the U.S. Department of State's Bureau of Intelligence and Research.

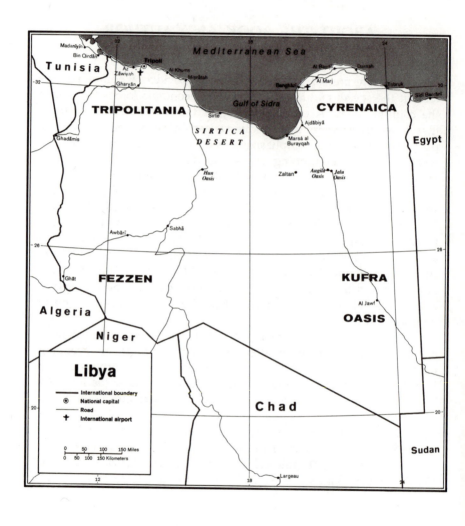

Madanīyīn
Bin Qirdān
Tunisia
Az Zāwiyah
Gharyān
Tripoli
Al Khums
Mişrātah

Mediterranean Sea

Al Bayḍāʾ
Darnah
Banghāzī
Al Marj
Tobruk
Sidi Barrānī

TRIPOLITANIA
Sirte
Gulf of Sidra

CYRENAICA

Ghadāmis

SIRTICA DESERT

Ajdābiyā
Marsá al Burayqah

Egypt

Hun Oasis
Zaltan
Augila Oasis
Jalu Oasis

Awbāri
Sabhā

FEZZEN

Ghāt

KUFRA

Al Jawf

Algeria

OASIS

Niger

Libya

—— International boundary
⊛ National capital
—— Road
✛ International airport

Chad

0   50   100   150 Miles
0 50 100 150 Kilometers

Sudan

Largeau

LIBYA

Qadhafi's Revolution and the Modern State

Lillian Craig Harris

© 1986 Westview Press

Westview Press • Boulder, Colorado

Croom Helm • London and Sydney

1986

Profiles/Nations of the Contemporary Middle East

Copyright © 1986 by Westview Press, Inc.

Published in 1986 in the United States of America by Westview Press, Inc.; Frederick A. Praeger, Publisher; 5500 Central Avenue, Boulder, Colorado 80301

Published in 1986 in Great Britain by Croom Helm Ltd., Provident House, Burrell Row, Beckenham, Kent, BR3 1AT

Library of Congress Cataloging in Publication Data
Harris, Lillian Craig.
  Libya: Qadhafi's revolution and the modern state.
  (Profiles. Nations of the contemporary Middle
East)
  Bibliography: p.
  Includes index.
  1. Libya. 2. Libya—Politics and government—
1969– . 3. Qaddafi, Muammar. I. Title. II. Series.
DT236.H375 1986   961'.204   86-13158
ISBN 0-8133-0075-4

DT
236
$.H375$
1986

British Library Cataloguing in Publication Data
Libya: Qadhafi's revolution and the modern state—(Profiles: nations of the contemporary Middle East)
  1. Libya—History I. Title II. Series
961'.204   DT236
ISBN 0-7099-3793-8

Printed and bound in the United States of America

∞ The paper used in this publication meets the requirements of the American National Standard for Permanence of Paper for Printed Library Materials Z39.48-1984.

10   9   8   7   6   5   4   3   2

To Marjorie Weaver Harris Cull
"Her children rise up and call her blessed"

Contents

Tables, Maps,
and Photographs

Preface

The two themes that dominate modern Libya are continuity and change. As a result of the 1969 revolution, the form and content of daily life have changed dramatically for all Libyans. Yet the influence of Libyan history and the pull of traditional culture remain extremely strong: The contest between the forces for and against change has not yet ended. Modern Libya may be extremely fluid politically, but it is much more inflexible sociologically. As few studies have been made of Libyan society since 1969, the facts are simply not all in. It would thus be folly at this stage in Libya's history to seek to provide absolute answers to a number of questions—including those concerning the ultimate effects and outcome of Qadhafi's revolution, Libya's future international role, and even the integrity of the Libyan nation itself.

Fortunately, a simple survey such as this does not have to be profound: It need only be as accurate as the available information will allow. My purpose, therefore, has been to provide a descriptive account—a briefing, if you will—on modern Libya's background and its present internal and international situations. I proceed from the premise that although Qadhafi's leadership is the central determining influence for change in modern Libya, the Libyan people continue by and large to resist radical change; for that reason, which is primary among all the others, the major goals of Qadhafi's revolution have not been achieved. My own bias is evident: Although the Libyan revolution has not been a total failure—its early goals of a heightened and more equitable national standard of living and greater authority over the country's oil wealth have been realized— Qadhafi's more ambitious goals for international influence continue to evade him, and the Libyan people continue to pay the price.

Any errors of fact and analysis in this study are mine alone. The statements in this book are not intended in any way to represent the official policy of the U.S. government or the position of the U.S. Department of State. It should be evident that they do not. This book goes to press just after the April 1986 U.S. air strike on Libya, an escalation by the Reagan administration of the U.S.-Libyan confrontation against which most U.S. government Libya analysts and regional specialists, including myself, have argued for several years. History will, as international opinion does now, condemn the U.S. action as counterproductive and conducive to further violence.

Lillian Craig Harris

Acknowledgments

In writing this survey over a period of months, I have had significant help from many friends and colleagues. Foremost among them is Jacques Roumani, whose article "From Republic to Jamahiriya: Libya's Search for Political Community" is a seminal study of modern Libya in historical perspective. Jacques read the entire manuscript in stages, making innumerable criticisms and corrections. In addition, I wish to express my deep appreciation to Lisa Anderson, to Marius and Mary-Jane Deeb, and to Dennis Murphy, who also read portions of the manuscript and provided valuable comments and criticisms.

A list of all those in the U.S. intelligence community, the U.S. foreign service, and the Washington diplomatic community who have helped clarify my thinking with rebuttal as well as agreement would be too extensive to include here. But among those who deserve particular thanks for provision of assistance and encouragement during the preparation of this book are David Long, George Harris, John Tinny, Ed Salazar, Roger Dankert, and Barry Rubin. My gratitude also goes to Nadia Rizk for assistance with bibliographic research while I was in Cairo during the summer of 1985, as well as to a number of Arab diplomats and government officials who would perhaps be embarrassed to have their names appear here but whose counsel and wisdom have been of particular benefit to me. To

Dr. Nicola Ziadeh, who first taught me about Libya when I was a student at the American University of Beirut, I am deeply indebted. Finally, I am grateful to my husband, Alan Goulty, whose encouragement, understanding, and love have sustained me.

1

Libya Through History:
Crossroads and Conquest

The story of Libya is one of successive invasions, of armies marching through sand from the east and arriving by ship from the north. Even the Berbers, usually regarded as the original Libyans, were invaders who probably arrived from Southwest Asia around 3,000 B.C. The earliest evidence of human life on the Libyan coastal plain—and in the areas to the south, which were eventually to become the great Saharan Desert—dates from around 8,000 B.C. Prehistoric rock art, painted and carved in profusion in some areas of Fessen and the Tibesti Mountains, illustrates the daily life of the Neolithic hunter, who sought animals now found only in tropical Africa.

The predominant themes of Libyan history are simple: repeated conquest from outside, followed by long periods of foreign dominance, and a lack of internal unity that rendered the region vulnerable to foreign attackers and exploiters. By the early years of this century Libyan nationalism had begun to emerge, but great differences of philosophy and aspiration, much of it based on regionalism, continued to divide the areas that would eventually be unified as Libya. The region of Tripolitania, including the important city of Tripoli and the surrounding areas under its control, looked seaward and, for long periods of history, toward the west for trade and cultural ties. Cyrenaica looked east and eventually came most deeply under Egyptian and eastern Arab influence. Fezzen looked south to black Africa.

In addition to successive invasions by outsiders and lack of regional unity, a dominant feature throughout Libyan history

1

has been the contest for power—usually won by urban dwellers—between coastal towns and hinterland tribes. The aspirations of the nomadic tribes of the hinterland were vastly different from those of the urban elites. This conflict between "the desert and the sown" has not been entirely resolved even today. Regionalism as well as the tensions between rural peoples and urban authority centers remain a feature of modern Libyan life.

An understanding of modern Libya would be impossible without some comprehension of the impact on today's Libyans of this history of domination by invaders and of the region's inability to unify. Their history of exploitation is held ever before their eyes by Mu'ammar Abu Minyar al-Qadhafi, who seeks to develop in the Libyan people a sense of colossal historical injustice for which they must be revenged—a sense probably deepened by the bedouin culture that infuses Libyan society. A great part of Qadhafi's original appeal to the Libyans was his stated determination to throw off the vestiges of colonialism and to replace those Libyan leaders who, through continued subservience to outsiders, had suppressed the country's free development. Qadhafi's desire to change the Libyans into actors, rather than those who are constantly acted upon, is a significant motivating factor in his international and domestic policy.

FROM THE PHOENICIANS TO THE TURKS

The history of the region that eventually came to be known as Libya was determined by its position as a crossroads between Europe, Africa, and the Middle East. Even before the twelfth century B.C., the Phoenicians had established ties with the three Punic towns of Oea (Tripoli), Labdah (Leptis Magna), and Sabratah. From that time as well dates the beginning of the two great trade routes that, until the early part of this century, funneled slaves and merchandise from Central Africa through Libya to the Mediterranean.

The earliest known documentation of Libyan history comes from the time of the Egyptian Old Kingdom (2700–2200 B.C.). In that era Berber tribes known as Lebu, from which the modern name of Libya derived, raided east into the Nile Valley. During the time of the Middle Kingdom (2200–1700 B.C.), the Lebu were eventually subjugated by the Egyptians. In 950 B.C., however, a Berber officer in the Egyptian army seized power and ruled Egypt as Pharoah Shishonk I. His successors in the twenty-second and twenty-third dynasties (950–720) were probably also Libyan Berbers.

By the fifth century B.C. Carthage had extended its control over much of the region of the three cities (Tripolis), holding a position of dominance until it was defeated by Rome in the Punic Wars (264–241 and 218–201 B.C.). Within a century following the final destruction of Carthage in 146 B.C., Tripoli had become a Roman colony. Cyrenaica, however, maintained ties with Greece and was colonized by the Greek states from the seventh century B.C. until the sixth century A.D. Within 200 years, Cyrene and four other city-states (the Pentopolis) were established. Among them was Berenice, later known as Banghazi. Fezzen, the third region of what was to become modern Libya, was loosely controlled by tribal people known as Garamentes from about 1000 B.C. The Garamentes conducted desert caravan trade from Ghadamis to the Niger River in the south, to Egypt in the east, and to Mauritania in the west.

Cyrenaica was subjugated by the Persians under Cambyses in 525 B.C. Following Alexander's death in 323, it was willed to Ptolemy and ruled from Egypt. Rome annexed the region in 74 B.C., and Cyrene continued its development into one of the intellectual and artistic centers of the ancient world. Septimus Severus, a native of Leptis Magna, rose to become emperor of Rome. He ruled from 193 to 211 during the 400-year period in which both Cyrenaica and Tripolitania remained Roman provinces.

In 429 the Vandals entered North Africa from Spain, establishing a kingdom with its capital at Carthage. The fall of the Vandal kingdom to the Byzantine general Belisarius in 533 led into a brief interlude of Byzantine rule. But political decay exacerbated by religious unrest—both Christianity and Judaism had been major religious forces in North Africa since the second century—presaged the coming change. The door to Arab invasion was left ajar.

Of all Libya's invaders the Arabs have had the most lasting impact, having grafted their religion and culture firmly onto the hardy Berber stock. In 642 Arab Muslims under Omar Ibn al-As conquered Cyrenaica and continued their sweep across North Africa. Germa, the capital of Garamentes, fell to the Arabs in 663. Conversions and cultural transmission followed as the conquerors settled in the area. But the impact of this first Arab group was not as great as that of the several even larger Arab waves that were to follow.

The Fatimid dynasty established in Egypt in 910 extended its control to Tripolitania. In 1049, however, the Berbers of Tripolitania revolted against the Shia Fatimids in order to restore Sunni orthodoxy. In a move that was to change the face of North Africa, the Fatimid caliph invited two large tribal groups from the Arabian Peninsula—the Beni Hilal and the Beni Salim—to quell his rebellious province. This time it was not warriors alone who moved, but entire tribes—up to 200,000 families entering North Africa via Egypt within a few months time. The eventual Arab character of Libya was thus ensured.

Meanwhile, the rival Berber dynasties known as the Almoravids and the Almohads had risen to power in Morocco in the eleventh and twelfth centuries. Tripolitania came under Almohad control in 1160, but Cyrenaica maintained ties with Egypt—sometimes lax, sometimes strict—for the next several centuries. Egypt was ruled by the Mamluks from 1171, when Saladin conquered the region, until the Turkish conquest of Egypt in 1510, when Cyrenaica, too, passed under Ottoman control. In that same year, however, Spain captured Tripoli, eventually turning it over to the Knights of St. John of Malta. Tripoli did not pass to Ottoman control until 1551, when the Turks drove out the Knights.

North Africa was never a central province of the Turkish Empire, and Ottoman control through the next three centuries was generally quite lax. Tripoli, Algiers, and Tunis—the three regencies in the Ottoman Maghrib—were subjects of periodic revolt and reextension of control. In 1711 a Libyan cavalry officer established the Karamanli dynasty in Tripoli—a manifestation of local autonomy that lasted until 1835, when direct Ottoman rule was restored. It took another twenty years to passify the northern regions definitively. Hinterland revolts continued into the 1860s, with some parts of the south escaping permanent Ottoman control altogether. By the middle of the nineteenth century, the Ottoman Empire was already in serious decline and, within a few years, would become popularly known as "the sick man of Europe."

The French occupied Algiers in 1830, and their eventual establishment of a protectorate in Tunisia (1881) was beyond the power of the Sublime Porte to counter. Meanwhile, with the opening of the Suez Canal in 1869, British interest in Egypt continued to grow. The Anglo-French convention that defined the British and Turkish spheres of influence in North Africa in 1890 in effect also established Libya—which had little to commend it where foreign colonization was concerned—as a sort of buffer between British and French spheres of influence. The stage was now set for Italy to grab a long-coveted piece of real estate.

THE FOURTH SHORE

Italy had been too weak and too disunited to join the European land rush between the sixteenth and nineteenth centuries. During the nineteenth century, waves of Italian emigrants, propelled by endemic problems of unemployment and over-population, left Italy, particularly for the United States. In 1896 the Italians' attempt to annex Ethiopia failed disastrously. The annexation of Libya, which at its closest point is only 350 miles from the tip of Italy's boot, seemed an attractive next step.

From 1907 on, the government of Italy adopted a conscious policy of "peaceful penetration" of the economic and social structures of Ottoman Libya. Having ascertained that the other European powers would not stop them, the Italians mounted an outright invasion in October 1911. Under the terms of a peace treaty with Turkey that allowed the Sublime Porte certain rights, including religious supervision, Ottoman troops were withdrawn from Libya in 1912. Yet, although Italy now had a free hand in Libya, the pacification process would take twenty years to complete.

By 1913 Tripolitania had largely fallen to the Italians, but this was to be the only immediate victory. An Italian invasion of Fezzen in the summer of 1913 led to capture of the major oases by early 1914, but at the end of that year Italian forces were driven out by bedouin resistance. Serious obstacles remained between the Italians and achievement of their aspirations. In April 1915 Ramadan Suwayhili, who was to become an anti-colonial hero, stopped cooperating with Italy and instead attacked, annihilating an Italian column near Sirte. By late 1915 the Italians held only a small coastal strip, and Suwayhili had established an independent republic with its capital at Misratah.

More important, there existed in Cyrenaica a popularly supported religious organization—the Sanusiyyah—that would effectively rally and lead the resistance for the next two decades. The impact of the Sanusi religious movement on modern Libya is difficult to overestimate. Begun in the Arabian Peninsula by Muhammed ben Ali al-Sanusi (1787–1859), the Sanusiyyah soon moved its headquarters to Cyrenaica, where a lack of political control—as well as a bedouin population in need of a guiding philosophy that structured but did not bind—was conducive to the growth of this fiercely independent religious order.[1] The first Cyrenaican *zawia* (hostel) was established in 1843 at Al Bayda. These compounds, containing schools, hospitals, and community centers, were soon established over much of Cyrenaica. In 1895 the headquarters of the order moved to Libya's Kufrah Oasis.

It is of major importance that the only significant national leader during the period of Libya's independence struggle against Italy was both Cyrenaican and Sanusi. Sayyid Idris al-Sanusi, who because of his position as leader of the Sanusi movement was eventually propelled into a position of national leadership, complained years later, after he had been deposed, that he had never wanted to be king but had only sought to do what was best for Cyrenaica.

The advent of World War I improved Italy's opportunity in North Africa. The April 1915 Pact of London promised to Italy all of the rights enjoyed by Turkey in Libya. Thus reassured, Italy entered the war in May on the side of the Allies. Despite support from Germany, Austria, and Turkey, Libyan resistance to the Italians was seriously weakened by Suwayhili's feud with the Sanusi. Nonetheless, following the war, political and economic difficulties at home focused Italian interests elsewhere and allowed at least temporary compromises with the Libyans. In 1917, through the good offices of Great Britain, a peace agreement was reached between the Italians and Sayyid Idris in Cyrenaica. Meanwhile, an agreement for self-government with some measure of Italian control was reached between Italy and Tripolitania. In 1918 the Misratah-based Tripolitanian Republic was declared. By 1920 the Italians, trusting their luck in an attempt to co-opt the Sanusi, recognized Sayyid Idris as the hereditary amir of Cyrenaica and thus accepted his authority over much of the interior.

These political successes for the Libyans, as well as the 1920 death in battle of Suwayhili (an enemy of the Sanusi), enabled the Tripolitanians to overcome their abhorrence of dealing with the Sanusi. The threat of fascism, moreover, encouraged a united front of nationalist forces against Italy. In 1922 a Tripolitanian offer to recognize Idris as the amir of all Libya was accepted. But knowing the move would result in Italian military action against him, Idris fled immediately to Egypt, leaving the resistance under the charge of Umar al-Mukhtar, an elderly but experienced fighter.

Mussolini's accession to power in October 1922 provided new impetus to the desire to form Libya into a "fourth shore" of the Italian homeland. Reconquest began in earnest in late 1922, and northern Tripolitania was quickly subdued. By 1928 Italy had conquered the Sirtica Desert, and in 1930 it pacified the Fezzen. Although resistance continued in Cyrenaica until 1931, during the final few years the cause was clearly hopeless in the face of Italy's superior firepower, search-and-destroy missions against nomad encampments, and scorched-earth policies. The death of Umar al-Mukhtar—who was finally captured and executed in September 1931—scattered the remaining fighters, and in January 1932 the pacification of Libya was officially announced. In 1937, at a ceremony in Tripoli, Mussolini had himself proclaimed the "Protector of Islam," and in January 1939 Libya (now divided into the four provinces of Tripoli, Misratah, Banghazi, and Darnah) was declared officially integrated into metropolitan Italy.

A pacified Libya next became the object of intense colonization. By 1940 approximately 110,000 Italians had emigrated

to Libya, where they constituted about 12 percent of the total
population. During the colonial period, which lasted until the
Italian authorities were driven from Libya during World War
II, Libya's economic progress was impressive, especially in the
area of agricultural development. In addition, public services
were greatly expanded, and public works such as roads, irrigation
systems, and port facilities were improved.

Such benefits, however, were enjoyed mainly by the settlers
and a very small class of upper-crust Arabs; those benefits
involving land use, especially, were carried out at the direct
expense of the Libyan Arabs. The administration, moreover,
remained totally in the hands of the Italians, and traditional
forms of government, including tribal councils, were abolished
in an attempt to prevent resistance. Even more serious for the
future of the country, no educational systems for Arabs were
set up and no attempt was made to train indigenous Libyans
to participate in the country's government or administration.

But just as World War I had smoothed the way for Italian
control over Libya, World War II brought that control to an
end. Once again, it was not the Libyans themselves but the
great powers who decided the outcome. Italy entered the war
in June 1940 on the side of the Germans, resulting in almost
immediate contacts between Libyan nationalists and British
authorities in Egypt. Groups of Libyans from both Cyrenaica
and Tripolitania sought out Idris, who was still in Egypt, and
expressed willingness to rally behind his leadership despite
continuing differences over the Sanusi factor. A conference of
Libyan leaders met in Cairo in August 1940, declaring support
for the Allies and granting to Idris the authority to negotiate
with Britain for Libyan independence.

Although the British publicly pledged that Italian domination of Cyrenaica would not be perpetuated after the war,
they remained noncommittal regarding the form that a postwar
Libyan government would take. Nonetheless, the Libyans assumed for the most part that independence—including independence for Cyrenaica and Fezzen—would be granted. For the
duration of the war, the Libyan Arab Force served under British
command.

The war itself was an experience that continues to scar the minds of many Libyans, who once again found themselves pawns in the hands of stronger international forces. For Qadhafi and many other Libyans, World War II is no mere historical event but a living reality that must be remembered and used. Thousands of Libyan Arabs, out of a total population of less than 1 million, were killed. The country's economic structure, such as it had been, was devastated. And Qadhafi, whose sense of history is infused with the bedouin idea of blood debt, to this day frequently repeats his demand that Italy and Britain pay reparations for damage to Libya during World War II. (The Libyan leader believes, in fact, that all of Libya's traditional oppressors must pay for their historical sins. For example, in a speech delivered on March 2, 1985, he once again castigated the Turks for turning Libya over to the Italians in the early part of this century.)

British forces, leaving Egypt under General Archibald Wavell, overran Cyrenaica in February 1941. Within a few weeks, however, the Italian defenders had been reinforced by the German Afrika Korps, which under Lieutenant General Erwin Rommel counterattacked strongly. During the next several months battles surged back and forth across the Western Desert, and in January 1942 a massive German offensive carried Rommel through Tobruk to within 60 miles of Alexandria before he was checked at Al Alamein. In October the British 8th Army under General Bernard Montgomery pushed through the German/Italian line, and by November Cyrenaica was once again in British hands. Tripoli was taken in January 1943, and by mid-February the last Axis forces were driven from Libya. From 1943 until the establishment of UN controls, Libya was governed by a British military administration in Cyrenaica and Tripolitania and by a French military administration in Fezzen. These administrations saw themselves as caretakers pending the end of the war.[2]

AN INDEPENDENT LIBYA

At the 1945 Potsdam Conference, the Allies decreed that the Italian colonies taken during the war would not be returned to Italian control. Although it was generally agreed that a trusteeship was the preferred form of government for Libya, no agreement could be reached regarding the form of that trusteeship or who would administer it. Finally, a suggestion from the British that Libya be given immediate independence was reluctantly accepted by France, the USSR, and the U.S. Under the terms of the February 1947 peace treaty, Italy renounced all claims to its former African possessions.

Nonetheless, final disposition of the Italian colonies was postponed for a year to allow the Allies to search further for a solution, failing which the matter of Libya's future would be turned over to the UN General Assembly. A Big Four investigation commission found the Libyans to be overwhelmingly in favor of independence but also questioned Libya's competence to engage in self-governance. In 1949 Idris, with British support, unilaterally declared Cyrenaica an independent amirate. The British motivation appears to have been a desire to thwart the pressure coming from the Soviet Union, which sought to persuade the UN that it be allowed to establish a trusteeship over at least part of Libya. Meanwhile, British Foreign Minister Ernest Bevin and Italian Foreign Minister Carlo Sforza reached agreement on a plan that called for a UN trusteeship over Libya, with British administrative responsibility in Cyrenaica, Italian in Tripolitania, and French in Fezzen—and independence to come ten years later. This plan, forwarded to the UN over Libyan protests, was endorsed by the UN Political Committee in May 1949 but was voted down by the General Assembly.

Something had to be done. In November 1949, a UN resolution calling for establishment of Libya as a sovereign state no later than January 1, 1952, was passed by a vote of forty-eight to one, with nine abstentions. A Council of Ten headed by UN Commissioner Adrian Pelt of the Netherlands was set up to administer the country during the transition period. Appointed to this council were representatives from the three Libyan provinces as well as from the United States, Great Britain, France, Italy, Egypt, and Pakistan. Pelt in turn oversaw the appointment of a Preparatory Committee of Twenty-One Libyans, who were to determine the composition of a national constitutional convention. Nonetheless, regional divisions continued to occur during the selection of the Cyrenaica delegates by Idris, those from Fezzen by the dominant Sayf al-Nasr clan, and those from Tripolitania by the Grand Mufti.

In November 1950 the National Constituent Assembly convened for the first time and approved a federal system of government presided over by a monarchy. The monarchy was offred to Idris, who accepted, and the United Kingdom of Libya was proclaimed on December 24, 1951. The colossal difficulties facing the new nation were remarked upon by the first U.S. ambassador to Libya, Henry Serrano Villard, who later wrote that at the time of independence only sixteen Libyans held university degrees and that the "political know-how" of the people was as "subnormal" as the Libyan economy.[3]

LIBYA UNDER THE MONARCHY

From the beginning, the Libyan federation was weak. The monarchy had sweeping powers that it frequently abused. The country's first general elections were held in February 1952, following which all political parties were dissolved and prohibited. Under the terms of the constitution, a bicameral legislature could easily be manipulated by the king: Idris had the authority not only to appoint half the members of the upper house (Senate) but also to dissolve the lower house (Chamber of Deputies) and to veto its legislation.

The ascension of a Cyrenaican Sanusi as king was a stumbling block to many Tripolitanians, and the government was plagued by disputes between the federal and provincial administrations. Tripoli and Banghazi alternated as national capitals in an effort to defuse regional tensions. In a further step toward strengthening national unity, Parliament in April 1963 passed a bill prompted by the king that abolished the federal government system and established, instead, a unitary monarchy with a dominant central government. The same measure enfranchised Libyan women and redivided Libya into ten provinces, each with a governor—thus abolishing on paper the three traditional national divisions.

Problems of royal succession were also a matter of dispute, particularly following the appointment of royal nephew Prince Hasan al-Rida as heir in 1953. In October 1954 a royal decree sought to squelch this dispute by limiting the line of succession to Idris's branch of the Sanusi family.

Politically, the new country found itself particularly dependent on Great Britain, with which King Idris had been in close consultation even before Libya's independence had been formally declared. In 1953 Libya signed a twenty-year treaty of friendship and alliance with Great Britain that included agreement for military bases. The United States, having also secured military basing rights, signed an agreement with Libya in 1954 for the major Wheelus Air Force base complex. Western military bases provided much-needed income to Libya in the early years of independence, but they were also a cause for concern among those Libyans (and other Arabs) who saw the danger of falling once again into a colonialist trap. In 1953 Libya joined the Arab League and, seeking to diversify its friendships, established diplomatic relations with the Soviet Union in 1955. Later that year Libya was admitted to the UN.

Despite an influx of technical, agricultural, educational, and other aid from the UN and from both the United States and Great Britain, Libya remained extremely poor during the first years of independence. In June 1959, however, the U.S. petroleum company Esso (which later became Exxon) confirmed the discovery of major petroleum deposits at Zaltan in Cyrenaica. By the mid-1960s, the freedom provided by growing indigenous income, combined with the increased appeal of Arab nationalism, prompted the Libyan government to seek evacuation of U.S. and British bases before the respective treaties expired. Although most British forces were out of Libya by 1966, the final evacuation of U.S. facilities was not complete until March 1970, by which time Qadhafi had come to power.

Yet the moves made toward elimination of foreign bases were not enough to stem the rising popular discontent. Corruption in the bureaucracy and misuse of the country's petroleum income came increasingly under public attack. In all probability, around the time of Qadhafi's successful coup on September 1, 1969, at least three other groups were also plotting the overthrow of the government: (1) senior army officers, (2) business and professional personnel, and (3) elements of the royal entourage—in particular the powerful Shalhi family, whose members included the chief of staff as well as a royal counsellor. Being neither Cyrenaican nor Tripolitanian but a bedouin from Sirte, Qadhafi, in some eyes, may have appeared to be an ideal leader for the rival regions. At any rate, he was seen as an honest and devout young man who could unify the country, turn it from corruption, and set it on a true Arab course.

QADHAFI'S COUP

Led by Qadhafi, the "Free Unionist Officers" who carried out the successful September 1969 coup had been plotting against the monarchy for almost ten years (see Chapter 3). Their leader was a 27-year-old captain in the Signal Corp for whom the 1967 Arab defeat, including Nasser's personal humiliation, had been a great shock. But that Arab disaster only reinforced the determination of Qadhafi and his fellows to restore Arab honor. Qadhafi's criticism of the Libyan government for failing to take a stronger stand in support of Egypt brought him increased support among his fellows and advanced the point at which the intricate and growing web of plotters, almost all of them in the military and most quite junior, would deem the time right to act.

Originally planned for March 1969, the coup was postponed several times. The March 12 plans were canceled because the popular Egyptian singer Um Kalthum was giving a concert in Tripoli for the benefit of the Palestinian resistance organization Fatah, a cause supported by Arab nationalists. Later that same month, and once again in August, plans were called off because of military intelligence investigations. Military and civil authorities, as well as at least one other group of coup plotters, appear to have been receiving at least fragmentary intelligence about the Free Officers and their intentions.

Despite growing urgency, the Free Officers were determined to await the fulfillment of three conditions they deemed necessary for success—namely, that all senior armed forces commanders had to be in the country, that King Idris had to be away from his support centers in Cyrenaica (as it turned out he was in Turkey for medical treatment), and that all members of the government had to be in one place. The coup was finally carried out on the night of August 31/September 1, just before several of the principal planners were scheduled to be transferred abroad for training.

Within only a few hours, the Free Officers working in small groups had occupied key government installations, including radio stations, airports, and police posts, in the three major towns of Tripoli, Banghazi, and Al Bayda. The army quickly declared its support, the police offered little resistance, and the popular response was one of enthusiasm. The Free Officers neutralized those few police and army personnel who resisted, and arrested government officials and members of the royal family. The final holdout was the city of Tobruk, which waited three days before satisfying itself that the monarchy had indeed been abolished and that declaration of allegiance to a new leadership was a requirement.

The success of the coup, its largely bloodless nature, and the widespread enthusiasm with which it was greeted were largely the result of popular dissatisfaction with the corruption and mismanagement that characterized the monarchy. Declarations of support for the Free Officers flowed in. And as dawn broke on September 1, Qadhafi, still unidentified, broadcast the first revolutionary bulletin from the Banghazi radio station. He claimed that the Libyan army had conducted the coup in response to "your incessant demands for change and regeneration" and in order to overthrow "the reactionary and corrupt regime, the stench of which has sickened and horrified us all."

A possible rallying point for the opposition was defused within a few days when Crown Prince Hasan al-Rida declared his support for the revolution and renounced all rights to the throne. Although Idris made an early attempt to persuade Great Britain to intervene on his behalf, popular acceptance of the new regime and almost overnight international recognition shortly persuaded him to accept assurances of the safety of his family in exchange for his agreement not to try to return to Libya. Not long afterward he retired to Egypt, where, though condemned to death by the Libyan regime in October 1971, he died of old age in 1983.

Qadhafi's September 1 proclamation extended guarantees of security to the representatives and property of foreign governments in Libya, and offered assurances that all treaties and agreements would remain in effect. It also made clear, however, that the new regime was Arab nationalist in orientation, committed to Islam and to domestic reform, and opposed to colonialism, imperialism, and communism. The revolutionary group's slogan "Freedom, Socialism and Unity" bespoke its Nasserite roots. Parliament was abolished, and a twelve-man Revolutionary Command Council (RCC) was established to govern the country.

Not until September 8, when Qadhafi was publicly promoted to colonel and appointed as commander-in-chief of the armed forces, did it become clear who the coup leader was. Until then a figurehead leader, Colonel Saad al-Din Bushwairib, had answered questions and undertaken the necessary public functions. Although analysts have hypothesized that Qadhafi's hesitation was motivated by security concerns, it is probably just as likely that his reluctance to rush forward represented an effort to demonstrate that power had changed hands by the will of the people and not by the manipulation of one man or even a group. It is also possible that, as with Nasser's 1952 coup, the members of the coup were in conflict over who would receive which position. Whatever the reasons, the names of the other eleven members of the Revolutionary Command Council were not declared for four months as the new regime began the daunting task of learning to govern a country.

The Early Years of Qadhafi's Rule

In proclaiming the Libyan republic on September 1, 1969, Qadhafi stated that his objective was to undo the acts that had "shattered our honor." He further pledged to expel the Italian Libyans; to evacuate the foreign bases, to achieve neutrality between the superpowers, national unity, and Arab unity; and to eliminate political parties (which had not, however, functioned in Libya since their abolition by King Idris in 1952). His more immediate economic measures included rent reductions, the doubling of the minimum wage, and conversion of foreign banks into Libyan joint-stock companies. In addition, Qadhafi ordered that all place and street names be rewritten in Arabic; he also banned alcoholic beverages, further restricted Sanusi activities, and closed non-Muslim religious institutions.

Stressing his own humble background as a man of the people, Qadhafi identified the Libyan "working forces"—upon whom the revolution would be built—as the peasants and other workers, soldiers, revolutionary intellectuals, and "non-exploiting national capitalists." Among these, members of the military were clearly the most important and ideologically the most "pure." As one scholar has pointed out, if Qadhafi had come to power proclaiming the Third Universal (or International) Theory, he almost certainly would not have retained power for very long: "As it happened, the theory evolved and Qadhafi's more radical policies were introduced gradually. Thus, despite the later imposition of eccentric policies, it is worth recalling that in its early stages the Qadhafi government followed fairly conventional Nassarist precepts."[4] Historian Ruth First described the RCC's hold on power as "the Nasserite precept of the hegemony of the military."[5]

Changes in the legal structures of the country came swiftly. In 1970 the RCC established a Legislative Review and Amendment Committee to bring laws into conformity with *sharia* (religious law) and to do away with the dual system of civil and religious courts employed under the monarchy. By late 1972 several criminal laws requiring Koranic punishments such as amputation had been passed. (On the other hand, there is no evidence that such severe laws had been applied since 1969.) At the lowest level of the judicial system, partial or summary courts were established. Cases appealed from these lower courts were to pass through courts of first instance and appeal courts before arriving at the supreme court. One aspect of the 1973 "cultural revolution" was to ensure the primacy of *sharia* over existing laws and practices, including strict adherence to *sharia* regulations banning alcoholic beverages and prohibiting the collection of interest.[6]

During the first year after the revolution, "people's courts" tried the former king (in absentia) as well as former politicians and journalists. Party activities were declared "treasonable" and labor unions became illegal, although new unions were then formed under government control. Women's associations and the lawyers' union were also dissolved. Within a year, intellectuals were falling silent in the face of reprisals against them for expressions of contrary opinion. In fact, the dust of the revolution had scarcely settled before Qadhafi revealed his clear intention to demand total acceptance of his ideas, even from the other Free Officers.

The early years of the Libyan republic were characterized first by acrimonious discussions in the Revolutionary Command Council and then by the gradual gathering of all authority into Qadhafi's hands as he moved to ease out of positions of authority or to disadvantage those who had come to power with him. A weapon frequently used against his opponents was the threat of resignation, which, because of his personal popularity, provoked demands that he stay on as leader. (It is noteworthy that as of the early 1980s, Qadhafi's resignation threats have usually been couched in more cautious terminology—that is, as offers to withdraw "if" there were no desire for him to continue, or as declarations that he would leave Libya "if" it were for the good of the people and they so decreed.) A civilian Council of Ministers established in 1969 was, itself, soon offering to resign, inasmuch as its authority had been co-opted by the RCC. In early 1970 Qadhafi and four other RCC members joined the council, but its composition continued to change rapidly such that in a two-year period there were four councils of ministers.

In May 1970 a ploy called the "Revolutionary Intellectuals Seminar" was begun in an effort to co-opt intellectuals to the cause of the revolution. But public discussions between Qadhafi and various groups of intellectuals alienated the intellectuals as Qadhafi refuted all ideas but his own. Newspapers were suspended in 1972 when Qadhafi and those in power around him recognized that censorship alone was insufficient to bring all thought into conformity with the goals of the revolution. The same year witnessed the first government-student confrontation, when students struck in protest over government interference in student organizations. And in March 1972 a dock workers' strike for better working conditions and higher pay at Tripoli harbor resulted in the outlawing of strikes and other public demonstrations against government policy.

In 1973 Qadhafi launched his Third Universal Theory, which posits that religion and nationalism are the driving forces of history. To implement the theory he also launched a "cultural revolution," the goals of which were (1) replacement of all laws by revolutionary laws; (2) the "weeding out of all feeble minds" by taking "appropriate measures towards perverts and deviationists"; (3) an administrative revolution to get rid of bourgeois and bureaucratic manifestations; (4) the setting up of people's committees to deliver power to the people and to take it away from bureaucrats and opportunists; and (5) the elimination of "all imported poisonous ideas."[7] Through the agency of the popular committees—which at this stage operated for only a few months before fading away—large-scale arrests were made involving those who either opposed the revolution or were not sufficiently identified with the new regime.

In the early 1970s, Qadhafi also gradually began to divest himself of official titles. An April 1974 decree relieved him of all political, administrative, and protocol functions so that he could devote himself to the development of revolutionary ideology. In 1976, having determined that the time had come for direct implementation of his political and economic theories, he resumed leadership of the RCC, announcing on the September 1 anniversary of the revolution that the RCC would be replaced by a General People's Congress. In the complex system of government that has evolved since that time, lines of authority overlap and blur as Qadhafi uses the competition for his favor on the part of various individuals and groups to his own advantage, both to maintain his ultimate authority and to ensure that no other individual constructs a viable power base.

Coup Attempts Against Qadhafi

Right from the beginning, Qadhafi has had to guard against violent efforts to drive him from power. The first of these occurred in December 1969, at the hands of the minister of defense and the minister of the interior, both of whom were arrested and charged with engaging in an "abortive plot." Then in July 1970, scores of people were arrested following discovery of a conspiracy headquartered in Sabha but said to be directed from outside Libya by royalist elements. Between 400 and 500 former high-ranking police and military officers were arrested and tried by people's courts. Most of the accused received relatively light sentences, and of those individuals sentenced to death, none were executed. In 1971 and 1972 some 200 former government officials and members of the royal family were tried on charges of treason and corruption. During this series of events, former King Idris was sentenced to death by a firing squad; but, happily for him, he was already living in Egypt.

What may have been the first really significant coup attempt occurred in 1975. By that time, despite the continuing popularity of social welfare programs at home and Qadhafi's apparently secure position as an important Islamic leader, it had become evident that the early promise of the revolution was not to be fulfilled. Disagreement with Qadhafi over economic management prompted RCC member and Minister of Planning Omar al-Meheishi to plot Qadhafi's overthrow. When one such plot was discovered in August, Meheishi fled from Libya. Qadhafi's betrayal by one who had been a member of his Free Officers and thus a member of the inner circle for a number of years marked the beginning of intense personal security measures and greater distancing by Qadhafi from the common people. The same year also saw an increase in both the degree of organization and the visibility of the Libyan opposition abroad as Meheishi among others joined the ranks of Libyans in exile.[8]

The Declaration of the Establishment of the People's Authority of March 2, 1977, which officially renamed Libya the Socialist People's Libyan Arab Jamahiriyya, was another turning point. The Revolutionary Command Council, which previously enacted legislation by decree, was abolished on that date, making way for the direct rule of the masses. (When the RCC was conclusively abolished, all of its remaining members were appointed advisers to the General People's Congress Secretariat, although neither Qadhafi nor any of the other RCC members was given a formal position.) From that date on, attempts to apply radical economic and political policies were significantly accelerated. Although the constitution of December 11, 1969, was not abolished or replaced, the March 1977 decree amended it significantly. All political parties—including, this time, even the Arab Socialist Union—were banned.

NOTES

1. Although Qadhafi himself partakes of many of the tenets of bedouin independence and the desire for religious simplicity that motivated the Sanusiyyah, he has moved carefully since coming to power in 1969 to ensure that the order, already disestablished by the Italians, did not revive as an alternate power base.

2. Useful and readable overviews of Libyan history may be found in Ruth First, *Libya: The Elusive Revolution;* John Wright, *Libya;* John Wright, *Libya: A Modern History;* Majid Khadduri, *Modern Libya: A Study in Political Development;* and *Libya: A Country Study.*

3. Henry Villard, *Libya: The New Arab Kingdom of North Africa,* pp. 4, 6.

4. Lisa Anderson, in a letter to the author dated July 22, 1985.

5. First, *Libya,* p. 121.

6. The Libyan judiciary thus became essentially responsive to the executive: Court officials are government appointees, and laws are broadly interpreted in keeping with accepted policies and ideology. The supreme court president as well as the supreme court justices are appointed by the General Secretariat of the General People's Congress. In the early 1980s revolutionary committees, particularly those at the local level, began to usurp some of the local courts' functions. In late 1984 one observer described Libya as a country in which "the law profession has been eliminated." See Omar Nasser, "Libya: Democracy of the Gallows," p. 14.

7. First, *Libya,* pp. 137–138.

8. Omar al-Meheishi was forcibly turned over to the Libyan authorities by the Moroccan security service in 1984 after almost ten years of largely ineffective efforts to rally opposition against Qadhafi. He is alleged to have been kicked to death by Qadhafi's lieutenants as Qadhafi waited in an adjoining room.

2

The Land and the People

GEOGRAPHY

Libya's physical geography and location have been determining factors in its history. A narrow fringe of coastal plain, running the length of the country's 1,075 miles (1,730 kilometers) of Mediterranean coastline, abuts with the Libyan Desert, the dominating feature of both ancient and modern Libya. The struggle to hold back the desert—or to live within it—has been pervasive. Libya is about two and a half times the size of the state of Texas, yet only 5 percent of the country's 680,000 square miles (1,769,000 square kilometers) are economically usable even with sufficient irrigation. It has no rivers and no true mountains except for the Tibesti massif, which rises over more than 9,840 feet (3,000 meters) near the Chadian border.

A tongue of the Libyan Desert, the Sirtica, reaches so far toward the Gulf of Sidra that the region known today as Libya has historically been divided, with the peoples of the west oriented in more modern times toward the culture of the Maghrib (Morocco, Algeria, and Tunisia) and those of the east toward the Mashrik (Egypt and the Arab East). On the northern coast as well, the sea scoops inland to form the Mediterranean's largest gulf, which spans approximately 345 miles (552 kilometers) between the headlands in Tripolitania and Cyrenaica. The Libyan government claims national sovereignty over the Gulf of Sidra along a bay closing line of 32 degrees and 30 minutes, taking its claimed boundaries at the farthest point a full 155 miles (245 kilometers) from the coast.[1]

Libya is both an Arab and an African country, a position critical to one's understanding both of the Libyan people's self-

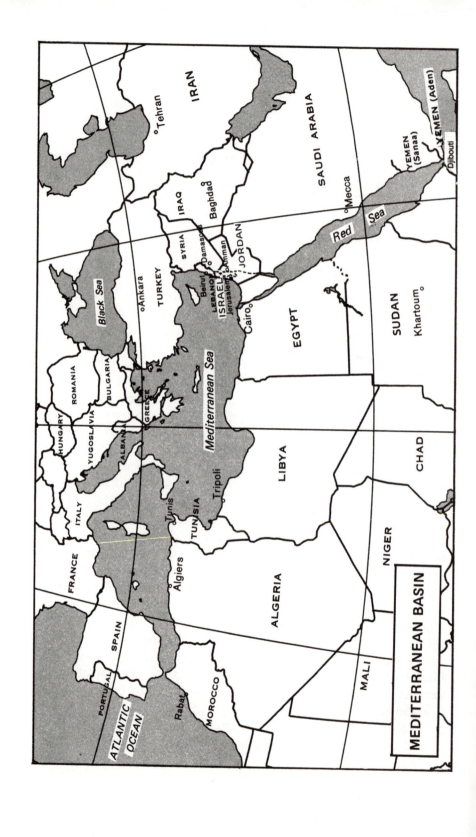

MEDITERRANEAN BASIN

image and of the political philosophy of their leader. Flanked by Algeria and Tunisia to the west and Egypt and Sudan to the east, Libya shares its 3,531 miles (5,650 kilometers) of frontier (including coastline) with the black African states of Chad and Niger. The desert separates the area into three major areas: Tripolitania (approximately 100,000 square miles, or 260,100 square kilometers), Cyrenaica (approximately 300,000 square miles, or 780,000 square kilometers), and below Tripolitania, Fezzen (approximately 280,000 square miles, or 728,000 square kilometers). The national boundaries are porous and, except where the desert is impenetrable, nomads have crossed at will for centuries. Disputes over the exact location of national boundaries continue periodically to trouble Libya's relations with each of its neighbors.

Despite the predominating desert, which itself comes in many forms and with a variety of vegetations, Libya is not a country of physical monotony. Although some 93 percent of Libya is desert, 6 percent is agricultural land and 1 percent is forested. Five climatic zones are identifiable: the coastal plain, with its humid maritime climate, which extends from Tunisia to Egypt and stretches 3 to 6 miles (5 to 10 kilometers) down toward Central Africa; the steppe country, which extends south of the maritime plain for perhaps another 12.4 miles (20 kilometers); plateaus in both Tripolitania and Cyrenaica in which the rates of rainfall are higher and snow is not uncommon; and the predesert and desert itself. The several great sand seas that spot the Libyan Desert are furnace areas in which men and animals die quickly of dehydration. By contrast, the desert also encompasses several important oases—Augila, Jalu, Kufra, Sabha, Ghat, and others—which include some of the country's best farmland.

Because of Libya's position between the Mediterranean and the Sahara, the country's climate is unstable and subject to sudden changes. The most dramatic of these is the *ghibli,* a hot desert wind (known as *hamseen* in the Arab East) that can occur during any season but comes most often between spring and autumn. A sharp drop in barometric pressure as well as extremely low humidity accompany the arrival of this withering wind, which brings with it a cloud of intrusive red desert sand. Such sand storms may last from a few hours to several days and then, with no warning, subside.

Not surprisingly, water and its sources have been of intense interest to both ancient and modern Libyans. The country's only lakes are small and salty, and rainfall is highly irregular, making farming and, in some areas, even life itself quite uncertain. An average rainfall of about 8 to 24 inches (200 to 600 millimeters) per year means that some areas go for years without rain, while in others cloudbursts fill the wadis with rushing water that further erodes the already abused farmland. Dams and water-conservation projects have received special attention since 1969, and misuse of water sources is a punishable crime. Most of the country's water is derived from wells and springs that tap the vast underground lakes, or aquifers, beneath the desert; the largest of these are located beneath the oases of Kufrah and Sabha. The Great Manmade River (GMMR) project (see Chapter 6) is the result of a modern and ambitious effort to tap these underground water sources.

FLORA AND FAUNA

In addition to its several oases, Libya's most productive agricultural areas are the coastal strip and the highland steppes just to its south—the areas in which some 80 percent of the population is concentrated. Productive farms eked out of the desert by Italian colonists in the 1920s, 1930s, and 1940s were allowed to deteriorate after World War II and during the early years following independence. Poor farming methods and erosion caused by overgrazing have taken a further toll. Although Libya does grow significant amounts of food—the main agricultural products are wheat, barley, olives, citrus fruits, dates, peanuts, and livestock—about 65 percent of Libyan food is imported.

In addition to domestic herds of goats, sheep, cattle, and camels, Libya has a variety of wild animals, most of them small and adapted to the desert. These include the desert hare, red foxes, jackals, hedgehogs, and a variety of rats including the long-legged Pyramid rat, or *jerboa*. Much less common in the years since firearms and aircraft were introduced are hyenas, antelopes, and gazelles. Libya's nonmigratory birds include larks, partridges, prairie hens, wild ringdoves, tufted bustards, and various raptors and vultures. As elsewhere in the developing world, the wanton killing of birds in Libya, including those on international migratory flights, takes a yearly toll.

The desert and coastal areas, too, feature a variety of smaller animals, such as snakes and scorpions. Coastal snakes— including the Green Snake, which grows to a length of four feet—are reputed to be harmless. The snakes of the desert include several specimens of the adder and viper families, which are highly poisonous. A variety of large poisonous centipedes appears to be native to Cyrenaica only, although it is believed to migrate occasionally to other parts of the country.

Along the coast and in the oases, Libya's vegetation is the familiar Mediterranean mixture of olive and fig, palm and fruit as well as deciduous trees. On the plateaus are fir trees, juniper, and cypress. A few miles inland, where the desert begins, the flora turns to short steppe grass interspersed with occasional wild olive trees and, after a rain, wild flowers. Here, too, the desert divides; hence certain species found in one region of Libya may be totally absent from another despite an apparently similar desert environment. Yet even this vegetation diminishes as the desert takes ever greater hold of the land. Finally, in the sand seas, there is nothing but occasional camel thorn and patches of almost microscopic plants with spore-like seeds that wait—sometimes for years—for the flash of rain that will bring them to a brief day or two of brilliance.

THE LIBYAN PEOPLE

A high birthrate and government encouragement for large families has raised Libya's population to over 3.5 million from just over 1 million thirty years ago. The first Libyan census, taken by the United Nations in 1954, revealed a total of 1,090,000 Libyans. The population is thus overwhelmingly young, with an annual growth rate in 1980 of 3.9 percent. Over half the Libyan population is urban, concentrated mainly in Tripoli and Banghazi. Some 50,000 Libyans are expatriates.

In recent years, the ethnic composition of Libya has changed with the departure of virtually all of the 30,000 or so Italians who remained in Libya in the 1960s. Also absent is the former colony of 35,000 Jews, most of whose ancestors had lived in Libya since Roman times. The majority of these Libyan Jews left after the establishment of Israel in 1948; the rest departed during or in the aftermath of the 1967 Middle East War. Libya's 1959 discovery of oil in exploitable quantities, however, resulted in an ethnic variety enriched by the influx of foreign laborers, experts, technicians, teachers, and others from Africa, Europe, North America, the Orient, and the Arab states. Libya contains a resident foreign labor force that fluctuates between 250,000 and half-million people, mostly from other Arab and Muslim countries. The largest groups of foreign residents are from Egypt, Tunisia, Pakistan, Turkey, Sudan, Syria, and India (see Chapter 5).[2]

Arabic for the Libyans is at once a language and a symbol. After the revolution, efforts to erase vestiges of colonialism and to renew pride in Arabism included campaigns to use Arabic on street signs, in newspapers, on shop signboards, as the sole language of educational instruction, and even in the personnel information sections in the passports of foreigners seeking to enter Libya. Literate Libyans read the universal classical Arabic but converse in Maghribi Arabic or in the Cyrenaican dialect more closely related to Middle Eastern Arabic, depending on the part of the country they come from. Neither the native schools nor higher Italian education were emphasized under the colonial regime; moreover, although older Libyans continue to understand Italian, it has been rejected in favor of English as a second language of instruction and technology.

Arabs and Berbers

Modern Libyans, though proud of their Arab heritage, are of mixed Arab and Berber stock. Perhaps the most racially "pure" Arabs of Libya are the Arab nomads, who descended from the eleventh-century Beni Hilal and Beni Salim migratory invasions. "Pure" Berbers, or those who speak Berber as their native tongue, today constitute only about 3 percent of the population, a much smaller percentage than those in Morocco, Algeria, or Tunisia. Although small Berber enclaves are scattered throughout Libya, most Libyan Berbers are found in Tripolitania's Jabal Nafusah highlands and in Cyrenaica around the town of Aujila.

Traditionally seminomadic, the Berbers were Islamicised by Arab conquerors from the seventh century onward (the process was relatively complete by the fifteenth century). The cultural vulnerability of the Berbers was accentuated by their lack of a written language and by the existence of several dialects. A further distinction is the adherence by most Berbers to the Kharidjite sect of Islam.[3] Since the Libyan revolution, government efforts to reduce tribal ties and to settle nomads have contributed further to the erasure of the Berber's special identity. Although nationalism has been used as a tool to overcome ethnic animosities, it is probable that Louis Dupres's 1958 observation remains true to a considerable extent: "Arabs in general and the patrician nomads in particular regard the Berber as an inferior creature. The Arab calls the Berber *Nafusi* and *Jabali*, once honorable names, but now the Arabs pronounce them with unmistakable scorn."[4]

Other Ethnic Groups

Only a few thousand Tuareg (the descendants of former caravan masters and raiders) remain in Libya. Sometimes known as "blue men" owing to the indigo dye in their clothing that infuses their skin, the Tuareg are Muslims with a strong admixture of native animism and African religion. Their culture places women in a high position compared to those in the traditional Arab cultures; that is, Tuareg women, not men, learn to read, inheritances are passed along the female side of the family, and men, rather than women, are veiled. Related to the Tuareg of Algeria and other parts of the Sahara, Libya's Tuareg are found mainly in the southwest desert near the oases of Ghat and Ghadamis.

The division of tribal regions, and of ethnic groups such as the Tuareg, by artificial national boundaries imposed on Africa by Europeans has provided Qadhafi a convenient rationale for irredentism. Because Qadhafi is of seminomadic background himself, and is thus inclined by culture to downplay the significance of national boundaries, the overlapping of tribal groups among Chad, Niger, and Libya has in past years fueled Qadhafi's call for a "Greater Saharan Arab Republic"—a viewpoint that, understandably, has alarmed the governments of Libya's weaker and more vulnerable neighbors.

Black Libyans. The descendants of former slaves, as well as of peoples who, in search of employment, have migrated to Libya from all over Africa in recent years, make up a sizable percentage of the Libyan population. Perhaps some 20 percent of all Libyans have Negro ancestors. In past years most black Libyans have worked as farmers, as sharecroppers, or, in urban areas, as menial laborers. Today many are employed in the petroleum industry, though seldom at the top levels given the continuing discrimination against blacks. Such discrimination, though not legal, is culturally ingrained. Black Libyans have also found a place in the lower ranks of the military, where (as in Chad) they have been used by the military authorities in Qadhafi's effort to convey the idea of racial solidarity with black Africa—or, in some cases, even to impersonate Chadian opponents.

The Tebu and the Duwud. Two other formerly significant ethnic/racial groups are rapidly disappearing. Of the Tebu, only about 1,500 persons are said to remain in the southern desert. Although their origin is unknown, they have been found to speak a language related to Nigerien. The Tebu are a small, dark-skinned people whose conversion to Islam is reported to have been diluted by continuing animism. The Duwud represent something of an ethnic curiosity. A few hundred of these negroid people remain in western Fezzen, where they are disdained by other Libyans for their choice of crayfish as a dietary staple.

LIBYAN SOCIETY

Tension between nomads and townspeople has been a feature of life since the time of the first human settlement. In Libya, dramatic differences of climate, topography, and cultural history have exacerbated these strains between the sedentary way of life on the narrow maritime plain and the harsh existence of the desert dweller. Libya, like Egypt, has been influenced by "the pull of the Mediterranean and the push of the desert." In addition to the city and desert dwellers of Libya are the rural dwellers—whether conventional farmers or seminomads who seasonally follow their flocks. These three basic ways of life continue to this day, though under changing patterns of population distribution, affected as they are by the rapid urbanization of recent years as well as by the cultural disruptions brought about by the pressures of modernization and the radical political philosophy of Qadhafi.

Yet, despite differences of life-style, the basic cultural values of Libyan society are similar for all three groups. The early Arab invaders brought with them a culture whose fundamental values had by the eleventh and twelfth centuries become Libyan values—and these have changed little to the present time. Libyan culture is Arab culture, with all the strong emphases on family and tribal kinships and the values of loyalty, solidarity, and faithfulness implied by that latter category. The primacy of Islam as a conveyer of that culture and the Arabic language as its expression is shared with all Arab countries. In Libya, Islam continues to play a central role in almost every aspect of daily life (as will shortly be discussed), and there are the expected sharp taboos of the Arab world against placement of personal before group welfare. Owing to the formerly isolated nature of Libyan society, many Libyans describe their culture as the most "pure" extant form of Arab culture found outside the Arabian Peninsula.[5]

Importance of the Cities

Despite the formative influence of the desert, the cities are the power centers in Libya (as elsewhere). The social and political organization outside the cities is generally limited to the level orchestrated by the government. Libya has only two major cities—Tripoli and Banghazi—although there are several other significant urban areas, such as Tobruk, Sabha, Beida, Misratah, Khums, and Zawiyah. As in many developing countries, even those blessed by ample natural wealth in the form of petroleum, the cities are frequently sites of overcrowding, insufficient housing, and, to an increasing degree, faltering social services.

Migration to Libya's cities basically coincided with colonization, but during the past three decades the movement of rural people and nomads into the cities has intensified as the cities have provided employment opportunities and a standard of living not available in rural areas. Nomads and seminomads probably constitute less than one-sixth of the current total population, and over 850,000 persons now live in Tripoli alone.

In an effort to prevent overtaxing of social services in the cities and a further reduction of the farming population, the Libyan government has adopted measures to keep rural peoples from flocking into the major urban areas. Since the revolution, it has also exerted considerable expense and energy in an attempt to settle the country's nomads, in the interests both of facilitating social services and of providing a method of political control. Entire tribes have been settled, entire villages moved. Redistricting has been carried out to obliterate regional and provincial divisions as well as local power centers. And local authority patterns and traditional institutions have been greatly weakened by division of the country into zones cutting across tribal boundaries.

Migration to the cities has resulted in the breakdown of certain traditional social norms, thereby contributing to what some have seen as an assault on "Arab values," others have seen as an opportunity for the liberation or license of women, and still others have seen as a destabilizing assault on the foundations of society itself. Thus traditional tribal and rural leaders, elected on the basis of family and tribal ties, have had their authority undercut not just by the appointment of public administrators but also by dislocation. Of pastoral origin himself, Qadhafi has well understood the deep roots of traditional authority patterns and the potential threat they pose to modernization as well as to his own tenure. Tribes, Qadhafi has said, are like political parties: Neither have a place in revolutionary Libyan society.

Libyan culture is nonetheless resilient; it resists radical change except among the very young. Despite the continuing large-scale movement into urban areas and away from cultural roots in nomadic or rural society, the basic cultural structure and values of traditional Arab society have been retained even in modern Libya's cities. The assault on tribalism as an institution notwithstanding, pride in tribal affiliation and lineage remains strong, even among those long disconnected from their nomadic roots. Indeed, the Libyans, including those whose grandparents migrated to the city, remain proud of their tribal and village ties.

Importance of Religion

For modern Libyans, just as for the Libyans from the time of the Arab conquest, Islam is the central fact of life. Modern youth may scorn certain laws or aspects of theology, but Islamic culture is pervasive and indelible. Religion and a religion-based culture infuse all aspects of Libyan life in much the same way that Christianity infused life in fourteenth-century Europe. Even for the secularized Libyan, there is no clear line between the secular and the sacred. All creation is God's work, and the chief duty of man is to submit to God and to the laws He has provided to guide man's way.

Thus Islam has been and remains the basic glue of Libyan society. As the primary unit of loyalty and identity, religion has been "a political symbol of crucial importance in controlling and mobilizing the masses"; it was also central to Arab League efforts to motivate Libyans to demand independence from the United Nations.[6] Even the forces that historically have pulled Cyrenaica toward the east and Tripolitania to the west are both basically the forces of Islamic culture. Although by the 1960s, independence, the oil revolution, and the forces of modernization had already "Libyanized" the people, Qadhafi—a man born in the desert near the central coastal town of Sirte—has since come closer than any Libyan leader before him to melding the Libyans into a national entity. Yet Qadhafi would be the first to admit that it is not any modern man or ideology that works to unify Libya, but Islam, the religion of God.

Most Libyans belong to the Sunni branch of Islam and adhere to the Malikite school of Islamic law, one of the four orthodox Sunni schools and the predominant one in North Africa. The Malikite rite holds that the Koran and the *hadith* (i.e., the sayings of the Prophet Mohammed) are the only primary sources of truth—as opposed to consensus (*ijma*) and analogy (*qiyas*), which are accepted by other Sunnis as legitimate sources. In keeping with orthodox Islamic belief, Libyan Muslims practice Islam's "Five Pillars": the profession of faith ("There is no God but God, and Muhammad is His prophet"), the giving of alms, prayer five times a day, fasting during the holy month of Ramadan, and the pilgrimage to Mecca. As with any religion, some who practice Islam in Libya are more observant than others. Moreover, certain conditions have traditionally excused some believers from observance of the pillars—for example, pregnant women and ill people in the case of fasting, and destitute people with regard to the pilgrimage.

The Religious Establishment

In traditional Libyan society, as in traditional Islamic societies everywhere, the lines between religious and secular power were thinly drawn. Both the caliph function of the Turkish sultan and the Sanusi leadership role that allowed Idris to become king illustrate the orthodox Sunni belief that God's authority is delivered unto one man who becomes at once both spiritual and political leader. In a unique way Qadhafi has benefited from this tradition to solidify his hold on power. Although he would deny that he seeks to be either spiritual or religious leader of his country, this combination of functions is evident in his leadership style. Qadhafi clearly regards himself as Libya's "Great Helmsman" (to adopt the phrase applied to Mao during the Chinese Cultural Revolution) and is not loathe to give religious as well as secular political advice. Moreover, although Qadhafi's three-part "Green Book" does not mention Islam, his religious orientation permeates this philosophical treatise.

In traditional Libya, the most powerful families were likely to produce the most powerful religious as well as secular leaders, further concentrating power in the hands of a few. It is not surprising, therefore, that Qadhafi's efforts to undermine the traditional power infrastructures of Libya have attacked the seats of both secular and religious authority. In the early days after the revolution, Qadhafi used the religious establishment to help legitimize his authority. Islamic canonical law, the *sharia*, was reconfirmed as the basis of the Libyan legal code and Islam was reconfirmed as the state religion. Sheikh Tahir al-Zawi was appointed "supreme spiritual leader" by the Revolutionary Command Council (again, witness the unity of secular and religious leadership), and both he and the Libyan Grand Mufti (the country's highest position of religious leadership) accompanied Qadhafi on a visit to France in late 1973.

Change was not long in coming, however. In May 1978 Qadhafi launched an attack on the religious establishment, during which his followers "liberated" mosques in several cities from imams and other religious leaders said to have deviated from true Koranic teaching. Many religious leaders and teachers were deprived of the privilege of speaking in mosques, and some, after several years, remain in prison (see Chapter 3). Under the revolutionary regime, particular antipathy has been reserved for those tribes and groups most closely associated with the Sanusi, from whose ranks the country's most recent leaders had been drawn. To undercut Sanusi strength in Cyrenaica, tribal lands not in use were confiscated by the state in the early days after the revolution. Various lands administered under the Islamic system of *awqaf* (religious endowment) were also confiscated.

The Changing Role of Women

The basic Libyan unit of society remains the family, including the extended family of clan and tribe. Society is male dominated along rigid authority lines, and the changing role of women in Libyan society is an interesting phenomenon in which the traditional values of female subservience vie with a revolutionary philosophy. Qadhafi has championed the cause of women's equality while at the same time revealing in his public statements traditional biases against full freedom for women. Nonetheless, real progress toward greater female equality has been made in Libya since 1969.

Traditionally, the Libyan woman—much like Arab women elsewhere—was considered inferior morally and intellectually. She was rigidly protected from contact with males who were not family members (although in rural and nomadic societies such segregation was considerably lessened by economic necessity), and she was considered responsible for the safeguarding of male honor. Virginity was guarded above all, and even rape was considered such a dishonor to the family that a raped woman could be killed. Real status as a person generally came to a woman only with the birth of a son. As a wife and mother she was expected to instill in her female children qualities of patience and endurance as opposed to qualities of aggression and forthrightness, which were encouraged in boys. Much of this traditional thinking is still evident in modern Libya.

After independence in 1951, and again after the revolution, laws were passed to protect women from arbitrary treatment at the hands of their relatives, including their husbands. No girl may be married under the age of 16 or against her will, and a woman may petition to gain legal permission to marry a man of whom her father disapproves. After 21, a woman need no longer petition the court but is free to marry whom she will—subject, of course, to the limitations placed on such freedom of choice by a family-centered society.

Under present Libyan law, no man is free to marry a second wife unless he obtains the permission of his first wife, and specific rights are guaranteed for divorced women. Although in Libya, as elsewhere, Islam allows a man four wives if he can treat them equally, the practice of polygamy has traditionally been more limited to Libya than in many other areas, mainly because of economic factors. Libyan law also prohibits the marriage of any male Libyan government employee to a non-Arab woman, an evident effort on Qadhafi's part to maintain security but also an interesting manifestation of cultural protectionism.

In postrevolutionary Libya there are greater opportunities for female education and employment, although society continues to channel women into the traditional social-service roles of teacher, secretary, and helper. Probably only about 5 percent of Libyan women engage in economic activity outside the home, although that number is growing as more women are inducted into the military. Most rural women, however, are involved in those traditionally unpaid economic pursuits considered essential to family income or survival. The Libyan Women's General

Union, created in an effort to address the problems of Libyan women in a changing society, became the Jamahiriyya Women's Federation in 1977 and has since then contributed to the advancement of women as an arm of government policy.

Society retains the means of circumventing the best-intended laws, however; and although Libyan women have advanced, most of them would not be considered free in the Western sense. Female freedom is limited by traditional ties to socially oriented careers for women and restrictions on movement outside the home. Moreover, the wide literacy gap between men and women reveals how many Libyan women must still marry a "superior"—a situation that has contributed to an increasing divorce rate as society becomes more modernized and men exposed to new wealth and opportunity seek to rid themselves of the traditional wives taken in their youth.

Social Revolution?

It is difficult to comprehend the problems faced by the Libyan people as they were being roughly trundled toward national identity and modernization over the past thirty years. In 1952, 90 percent of the population was illiterate. There was no tradition of Western-style self-rule and so little sense of national unity that under the monarchy it was necessary to designate both Tripoli and Banghazi—and later Beida as well—as co-equal national capitals. Even now, more than thirty years later, a clear sense of Libyan identity has not fully evolved in all sectors of society. Despite the breakdown of certain traditions and strictures, tribal and village group loyalties compete with feelings of nationalism and, in many cases, would still certainly win out if a choice became necessary.

The absence of a strong sense of national identity may lie at the root of what some have criticized as political lethargy on the part of many Libyans—at times an almost incredible passivity in the face of Qadhafi's assault on the country's religious and social traditions. Others attribute this phenomenon to lack of political sophistication. Nonetheless, despite widespread and at times massive disruption of traditional life-styles, popular passivity—contributed to by uncertainty, alienation from government, and the amenities of modernization—has been a continuing social phenomenon. For instance, large groups of Libyans welcomed the 1969 revolution, but when its promise failed they did not react violently. And now, in the mid-1980s, antagonism toward Qadhafi and his programs is growing, but surprisingly little overt opposition has been expressed toward Qadhafi's radical social and economic programs, and no large-scale uprisings against the regime have occurred.

Such passivity, however, works both ways. The 1973 Libyan "cultural revolution" was an attempt by Qadhafi to shake the people out of their political lethargy and to inspire a greater desire to work for the good of society and the country as a whole. But despite the lip service paid Qadhafi's cultural revolution, it was largely disregarded by the populace. Most Libyans remain reluctant to involve themselves in government affairs that can easily become detrimental to personal interests. Their usual response to political pressures appears to be a deepened interest in the private affairs of the family and immediate circle—that is, a reinforcing of traditional values. Despite Qadhafi's application of radical political theory in an effort to achieve national cohesion and to undercut potential opposition to the regime, Libya remains among the most conservative of Arab societies.

In the new Libyan society, which increasingly appears to be stagnating as a result of the application of Qadhafi's political, social, and economic theories, several basic social issues remain unresolved. In addition to changing patterns of authority and the role of women, these issues include the following:

- the pressures of urbanization, modernization, and Western culture on traditional society;
- the impact of dependence on the thousands of migrant workers (including the implications of living in a society in which the Libyans themselves are growing unused to manual labor);
- a critical "brain drain" as intellectuals leave the country;
- the difficulty of dealing with the inevitable personal fears that arise from living under a regime in which internal

repression and the possibility of external retaliation are always present; and,

- the problem of popular passivity itself—a question that has taxed even Qadhafi's resources for enthusiasm.

PROBLEMS OF THE WELFARE STATE

The transformation of Libyan society owes more to the discovery of oil than to the 1969 revolution. It is difficult, however, to conceive of the latter in the absence of the support of the former. In the early days of the monarchy, poverty was a major obstacle to nation building. In 1954, however, five foreign oil companies began exploration in Libya, and within a few years petroleum income had begun to change the country. Under the monarchy, an unwieldy bureaucracy, lack of trained personnel, inexperience, and corruption all inhibited efforts to achieve equitable distribution of the new oil wealth. A major factor in Qadhafi's initial support and popularity was his promise to end exploitation and his success in raising the standard of living by extending the benefits of national prosperity to all.

Following the revolution, Libya became a land of free social services. Education, health care, child care, unemployment compensation, and other benefits became available to people who had never dreamed they would be able to afford such luxuries. But as Qadhafi sought to implement what he called "Islamic socialism," and as he aimed toward "collective ownership" of property, it became clear that the country's human resources were not being equally developed. In subsequent years dramatic efforts were made to create agricultural, industrial, and economic infrastructures—as well as social-service systems. Yet it has become evident that nationalization, government control, and a radical ideology are not adequate to control certain very serious problems.

Among the most urgent of these difficulties has been stagnation in agricultural development due to the flow of rural people to the cities, where greater benefits of wealth and modernization are available. The eviction of Italian farmers, which began after World War II and accelerated following independence, also set back agricultural development. Despite efforts to entice rural peoples to remain in the country, Libya began a steady drift toward greater reliance on imported food.

Another difficulty is related to the appearance of the new elite, which still frequently finds itself out of step with traditional society. Only two of the twelve original members of the Revolutionary Command Council were members of powerful tribes; on the contrary, most were from poor families and noninfluential groups. The coming to power of these RCC members turned the world upside down for many Libyans, bringing as it did a new political and social elite heavily concentrated in the military and among the young. But this new leadership is not truly representative of Libyan society, which has clung to its traditional values.

Since the revolution, the educational system has been used by the government to further national unification efforts and to draw the Libyan people along the paths of modernization and support for government political programs. Impressive success has been achieved in the expansion of compulsory education from six to nine years, in the greater emphasis on technical education and the applied sciences, in the expansion of educational facilities to rural areas, and in adult literacy programs. After the revolution a new university was established in Beida, and Tripoli University (now Al Fatah University) and Banghazi University (now Qar Yunis University) have been expanded. Approximately 12 percent of the national budget is currently expended on education, which is free to students through the university level. Literacy is probably about 70 percent for males and perhaps 35 percent for females.

Nonetheless, serious problems remain in the educational system—problems that prompt serious questions about Libya's political and social future. Among them are the lack of qualified teachers, the absence of a consistently integrated curriculum, too many non-Libyan teachers, nonattendance by females, inadequate educational facilities, and traditional resistance by rural people to education, particularly education of women. Moreover, during the past several years, the regime itself has seriously disrupted the educational system by closing all private schools (1977), by seeking to integrate religious with secular education, and by imposing compulsory military service during primary and secondary education. Qadhafi's efforts beginning in 1984 to implement his plans to center primary education in the home could further damage prospects for sound basic education in Libya.

Among the other serious difficulties related to education is the continued shortage of technically trained personnel, despite governmental attempts to emphasize technical education. According to Marius Deeb and Mary-Jane Deeb, "There is undoubtedly a bias in the school and the university curricula of Libya as well as in those of other Arab countries toward an academic rather than a practical education."[7] Perhaps 90 percent of all medical doctors and dentists and 80 percent of all pharmacists in Libya are non-Libyan. The lack both of adequate long-range economic planning and of a consistent economic, political, and social philosophy has also taken a toll. Neither under the monarchy nor after the revolution has Libya been able to buy time for modernization.

Qadhafi's restrictions on free enterprise, commerce, and other forms of "capitalism" were intended to demonstrate to the people that they were "partners, not slaves." No one was to have more than he needed for his daily life, for, according to Qadhafi, "the legitimate purpose of the individual's economic activity is solely to satisfy his [material] needs." The result has been conflict between economics and politics. Major businesses, industries, and service organizations as well as the country's utilities, communications, and banking systems were all taken over by the government: According to Omar El-Fathaly et al., "The economic changes were accompanied by deep imbalances in the society. . . . The social environment, traditions, and customs matched neither the new economic conditions nor the new political arrangement. Political leadership deterred the public from real involvement in the affairs of their society."[8]

The elimination of individual traders and business people has been as much a blow to individual initiative as to the development of a true middle class. Early takeovers of industries and businesses by workers led to greater inefficiency and even a reinforcement of the perennially heavy-handed Libyan bureaucracy. In subsequent years the bureaucracy itself came under attack as Qadhafi sought to undercut all alternate leadership or power bases. In an August 1984 speech, for instance, he lashed out at what he described as "the new bourgeoisie . . . a phenomenon hostile to the masses' society." He also accused the members of this "bourgeoisie" of "occupying marginal posts, enjoying salaries, privileges and free goods without giving in exchange any significant productive work."

Such policy has had the effect of contributing to continued lethargy and lack of popular initiative. The welfare state—with its free services, subsidized food, inexpensive housing, social security programs, and medical and educational benefits—has greatly improved the lives of the people. But Libyan society has increasingly become one in which lack of incentive is rewarded and initiative, particularly of the political or economic sort, can mean trouble. The family-centered philosophy and traditional worldview that characterize this society have prevented expansion of intellectual and professional horizons. And despite the availability of free education, the initiative to take advantage of technical training is inadequate among most Libyans, who show little inclination to move beyond the white-collar professions that traditionally brought family prestige.

Modern Libya has been described as a *rentier* state—in other words, a country that receives revenue from the production and export of raw material that has little or no connection to domestic economic growth. As El-Fathaly et al. have noted, "The rentier state can achieve dramatic rises in per capita income without going through the social and organizational changes usually associated with the processes of economic growth."[9] So long as a high rate of national income was available to continue this way of life, particularly as the majority of Libyans over 30 remembered the days when they were much less well off economically, the government's economic and social policies were not seriously challenged. But as a result of the critical changes that have occurred in the world petroleum market in the early 1980s, the picture has apparently begun to change.

No definitive study has yet been made of the impact of the Libyan revolution on popular culture and social values. Clearly in progress, however, are several dramatic changes resulting from the dictates of ideology, the demands of modernization, and the opportunities of new national wealth. The revolution's assault on traditional authority patterns and the displacement of traditional leadership elites cannot help but eventually have a profound effect on traditional culture itself. Like many other developing countries, Libya is passing through a transition period in which basic values are being questioned. What remains unclear is just where Libyan society is headed. More apparent is the fact that seventeen years of a radical regime, growing popular disappointment over the failed promise of the revolution, and a youthful population do not necessarily promote prospects for stability.

NOTES

1. Burkina Faso is the only other country that recognizes this claim—a position of contention between Libya and the United States that contributed to military confrontation between the two nations in 1981 and again in early 1986.

2. The expulsion from Libya in 1985—for ideological and economic reasons—of approximately 60,000 expatriate workers affected mainly Tunisians and Egyptians.

3. The Kharidjites believe that any Muslim, not just an Arab believer, is eligible to become caliph and may be so elected by the community. Adoption of this sect by North African Berbers in the period following the Arab conquest was, in effect, a form of resistance to domination by the Arabs.

4. Louis Dupres, "The Non-Arab Ethnic Groups of Libya," p. 35.

5. Some eastern Arabs dispute this Libyan claim to cultural purity, citing what they regard as the lack of traditional Arab hospitality among Libyans owing to the "un-Arab" cultural trait of a more private home life and greater suspicion of strangers.

6. See Omar I. El-Fathaly and Monte Palmer, *Political Development and Social Change in Libya*, p. 26. Other helpful works on Libyan society include Omar I. El-Fathaly, Monte Palmer, and Richard Chackerian, *Political Development and Bureaucracy in Libya*; Marius K. Deeb and Mary-Jane Deeb, *Libya Since the Revolution: Aspects of*

Social and Political Development; and J. A. Allan, *Libya Since Independence: Economic and Social Development.*

7. Deeb and Deeb, *Libya Since the Revolution,* p. 45.

8. El-Fathaly, Palmer, and Chackerian, *Political Development,* pp. 27–28.

9. Ibid., p. 18.

3

Qadhafi:
The Man and the Leader

An understanding of the motivations, personality, and philosophy of Mu'ammar al-Qadhafi is essential to an understanding of modern Libya. It is Qadhafi's ideas that permeate the country and his fervor that has propelled Libyan domestic and foreign policy since the revolution. Without Qadhafi Libya would be a very different country socially, economically, and politically. Certainly, without him Libya's foreign relations would be much different.

But Qadhafi is a man about whom relatively little is known, a man who hides secretiveness behind flamboyance, whose paradoxes are many. Qadhafi is an intensely private individual; his quiet, even ascetic, domestic style contrasts sharply with his aggressive political behavior. Some—including a few Arab leaders—have called him mad. Others believe he has *baraka*, a quality of personality that goes beyond charisma into the realm of the mystical.

As usual, the answer probably lies in neither extreme. Qadhafi is indeed a man possessed of special abilities of rhetoric and persuasiveness, of vision and compulsion. But more than this, he is a product of his environment. The heritage of Libya's past under Italian fascist colonialism, the influence of desert bedouin culture, and the tenets of Islam have all molded his worldview. The most potent personal and political force in his early life was Gamal Abdel Nasser, whose 1952 authorship of the Egyptian revolution fired the young Qadhafi to commit a similar feat in Libya several years later. But Qadhafi is not a

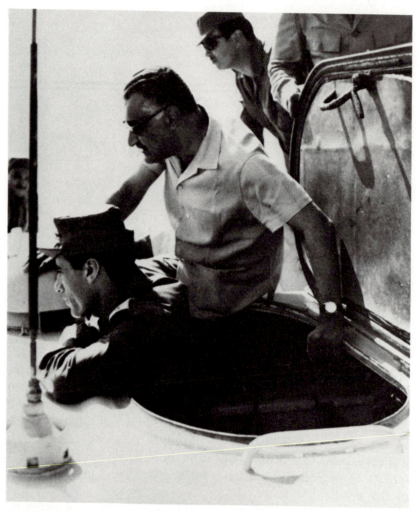

Qadhafi and Gamal Abdel Nasser inspect an Egyptian tank during a visit to an Egyptian unit in the field. Photograph courtesy of UPI/Bettmann Newsphotos.

mere mimic. Nor is he simply the product of his social, cultural, and religious background. His many-faceted personality has produced a unique and even extraordinary individual infused with a sense of divine mission and the determination to achieve that mission no matter what the cost.

QADHAFI'S YOUTH:
HOW THE TWIG WAS BENT

Mu'ammar Muhammad Abu Minyar al-Qadhafi was born in Sirte, Tripolitania, in 1942.[1] Because his parents were nomads, Qadhafi was born in a tent and grew up in poor surroundings. The small Qadhaafa tribe, of Berber stock (albeit Arabized), is proud of its tradition of being descendant from the Prophet Mohammed. The Qadhaafa have holdings in the Hun oasis, where as a child Qadhafi herded the family flocks, spending great amounts of time alone. His first formal education was Koranic: Through careful financial juggling, his parents—Abu Minyar and Aisha al-Qadhafi—managed to send him to a Muslim elementary school. Looked down on as a rustic bedouin by many of his classmates, the young Qadhafi is said to have slept in a mosque at night, returning to the family encampment on weekends. Qadhafi's father, who had fought against the Italians before independence, was a traveling merchant and presumably gone a good deal of the time. His son, the only boy of three children, grew up in a mainly female household.

In light of the permissiveness that characterizes the rearing of male children in the Arab world, the stage was set for the formation of a self-righteous personality positioned firmly against authority. Tales of Italian atrocities during the colonial period, the horrors of World War II fought on North African soil by outsiders, the 1948 shock of Arab defeat in Palestine, and the thrilling news of Nasser's overthrow of King Farouk in 1952 made deep impressions on the youth, many of whose early teachers were Egyptians. He listened avidly to the "Voice of the Arabs" radio program from Cairo, and Nasser became his hero and apparently one of the few people capable of influencing his opinion.

Qadhafi claims that he began to plan the overthrow of King Idris while still a school boy. Although accounts differ regarding the precise point at which he became an activist, it was probably around the time of the 1956 Suez crisis that he organized students against the Anglo-French-Israeli invaders and in support of Nasser's efforts to expel them. Certainly by the age of 15 Qadhafi was listening to Nasser's speeches and discussing them with his classmates. Among these boyhood friends were several who subsequently participated with him in the overthrow of Idris and continue to serve in the Libyan government, including Ali al-Houdery, expelled from Washington as head of the Libyan people's bureau in 1981; Abdel Salem Jalloud, who has been regarded for many years as the Libyan "number two"; Mustapha al-Kharoubi, commander of the Army Inspector General Corps; and Abu Bakr Yunis Jabir, Libyan army chief of staff.

From the time he was a schoolboy, Qadhafi's powerful personality enabled him to surround himself with like-minded followers whose desire to "free" Libya focused on the overthrow of the king. The Free Officers movement that eventually emerged from the youthful plotting of Qadhafi and his comrades was inspired by the ideals of both Egyptian Nasserism and Syrian Ba'athism. There was, moreover, a holy fervor about Qadhafi that made him particularly attractive to his fellow officers. Sent to the airport to meet *Al-Ahram* editor Mohamed Heikal—who had come as Nasser's envoy to see what the Libyan coup was about—RCC member Mustapha al-Kharoubi said of Qadhafi, "You can't imagine how pure he is." Having met Qadhafi, Heikal later described him to Nasser as "shockingly innocent" and "scandalously pure."[2]

During his third year as a student at Sabha High School in Fezzen, Qadhafi—who had formed a "Central Committee" and was holding secret meetings with his classmates to discuss Nasser's political ideas—was expelled for leading a student demonstration. Thereafter, Qadhafi studied in Misratah, either attending a school there or studying under a private tutor. He completed his secondary studies in 1961 or 1962 with no particular distinction, although he did develop a deep interest in history. In the following two years, which he spent studying history at the University of Tripoli, his worldview was expanded, but he ultimately failed academically and departed from the university.

As a youth, Qadhafi was once publicly slapped by a teacher. That incident may have contributed to his belief that no one should ever be forced to learn anything against his will; it may also have developed in him an ambivalent feeling about education in general. His youthful inability to come to terms with the academic environment continues to color Qadhafi's philosophy and actions. Although by Libyan standards Qadhafi is well educated, he frequently displays disdain for professors and "intellectuals" in general. In his speeches Qadhafi sometimes singles out teachers for particular criticism, defaming them as persons who have an enormous self-regard and yet misguide others.

At the first general meeting of Qadhafi's "movement," held in 1963 and attended by followers from Sabha, Misratah, and Tripoli, it was decided that Qadhafi and two others would enroll at the Banghazi Military Academy as a means of infiltrating the army and recruiting support for a coup. Today Qadhafi claims that this decision reflected his assessment that political change was possible only by military means. The actual extent of his involvment in coup-plotting activities at the time he joined the military is unknown, but certainly his plans were not highly evolved and most likely constituted little more than wishful thinking.

Qadhafi graduated from the Libyan Royal Military Academy in 1965. Before graduation he received some training at a military school in Turkey and immediately upon graduation was sent to the United Kingdom for advanced communications training. At Beaconsfield, a British Army training academy in Buckinghamshire, Lieutenant Qadhafi spent several months learning British signal corps techniques, which he later found useful in planning and executing his coup. Reports that Qadhafi had at one time attended a military training institute in the United States are untrue; they appear to have arisen from the theory—widely held in some Arab circles—that Qadhafi is actually the most clever CIA agent of all, created by the United States to divide and humiliate the Arabs.

QADHAFI AND RELIGION

Colonel Qadhafi's vision of himself is not complex. He appears to see himself as a simple revolutionary—a leader to be sure, but basically a pious Muslim called by God to carry out the mission that Nasser began but left unfinished by his early death. Nasser's vision of the concentric circles comprising the Arab, Islamic, and nonaligned worlds provided the projected arena for Qadhafi's establishment of a just society in accordance with the political principles expounded in his three-volume "Green Book." Included in this vision is an understanding of himself as an African as well as an Arab, a man destined to bring truth and freedom to black Africa as well as to the Arab states. Qadhafi's preferred title, "leader of the revolution," reveals the central position he ascribes to himself despite his formal renunciation of all official titles. Having in subsequent years undercut all alternate leadership bases in the country, Qadhafi jealously guards his own preeminence.

Religious faith is the central element in Qadhafi's psychological motivation. Yet despite his devoutness, he regards Islam as a tool, rather than government as an instrument of Islam—a point that has been a critical issue in his controversy with Libya's traditional religious leadership. Although Qadhafi defines his ideology as "Islamic socialism" and promotes the belief that the Koran contains all truth and wisdom, including scientific knowledge, he has, in fact, long been in conflict with Libya's religious establishment. The creation of the Arab Socialist Union as a mass organization in 1971 was intended to provide a single vehicle for popular political participation and representation. The traditional religious hierarchy had no clear place in this system and continued to function as an alternate source of authority. Nonetheless, it took some time for the new regime's controversy with the religious establishment to come to a head, as in his first few years in power Qadhafi was still preoccupied with working out exactly what his philosophy was.

In October 1977 an article that may have been written by Qadhafi himself appeared in the official newspaper *Al-Fajr Al-Jadid*, attacking representation of the people by religious functionaries. Shortly afterward, the Grand Mufti of Libya, Shaykh

Tahir al-Zawi, resigned his post and was not replaced. Then, in early 1978, the "people's committees" were ordered to seize those mosques exhibiting "paganist tendencies" and to cast out the "heretical imams." In a strong sermon at a Tripoli mosque in February, Qadhafi himself warned the *ulama* (religious notables) against opposing the regime.

The authority and position of the religious leaders was further eroded by a real-estate law of May 6, 1978, which undermined the traditional Islamic religious endowment system, the *awqaf*. In July, during a well-publicized discussion between Qadhafi and the *ulama* from throughout the Muslim world, Qadhafi stated his position that the *hadith* is not necessarily binding—an essentially heretical position and one that subverts the *ulamas'* interpretations of those sayings.

But Qadhafi's quarrels with the Libyan religious establishment are not solely based on his desire to eliminate the traditional religious leadership as an alternate source of authority: The Libyan leader is anticleric in part because he sees the Islamic clergy as impeding man's access to God. For Qadhafi, the Koran is a living document that must be interpreted and understood in light of contemporary history and events. In a particularly Protestant fashion, he has held that man needs no mediator between himself and God, just as he needs no ruler between himself and authority—that under true religion and true democracy, all are free. As evidence of his conviction that Islam is a living religion that provides responsibility to the individual, Qadhafi in 1979 officially revised the Islamic calendar, taking the Prophet's death—rather than the date of the *hegira* (the move from Mecca to Medina)—as the beginning of the Islamic era.

Qadhafi's attack on organized religion has been regarded by the more legalistic and traditionally minded as an attack upon orthodox theology. In the past few years, as relations between Colonel Qadhafi and the Libyan religious leadership have gradually worsened, Qadhafi has been accused of substituting the "Green Book" for the *hadith* (in social as opposed to ethical or divine matters) and even of placing his own ideas on a level with the Holy Koran—thus committing the heinous sin of *shirk* (idolatry), in the sense of ascribing knowledge to other than God.

Some pious Muslims have criticized Qadhafi as a heretic or a fanatic, then—but few have described him as insincere. At the crux of Qadhafi's religious faith lies the crossroads where the will of God and man become one: Allah expresses himself through Qadhafi, and Qadhafi's will is Allah's will. Those who oppose Qadhafi oppose God himself. In a 1979 interview with Italian journalist Oriana Fallaci, Qadhafi demonstrated the extent to which he believes himself a conduit for divine truth, claiming that "the Green Book is the guide to the emancipation of man. The Green Book is the gospel. The new gospel. The gospel of the new era, the era of the masses. In your gospels it's written: 'In the beginning there was the word.' The Green Book is the word. One of its words can destroy the world. Or save it. The Third World only needs my Green Book. My word."[3]

QADHAFI'S PERSONALITY

While it is always dangerous to attempt to analyze someone from another culture, several of Qadhafi's motivations seem almost self-evident. He is driven by anger over Libya's colonial past and has identified himself so completely with Libya that the country's past humiliation has become his own and vice versa. He has, moreover, a truly bedouin thirst for revenge against those who have humiliated him. Indeed, bedouin culture has influenced him in many ways, contributing as it has to his sensitivity to slight, his philosophy that the tribe—or extended family—is the basic unit of society (an evident contradiction given his attacks on the tribal structure), and his failure to accept internationally agreed boundaries. Even a cursory reading of the speeches Qadhafi has delivered over a period of years and a brief look at his activities will reveal a virtual catalog of psychological needs that appear to motivate the Libyan leader:

1. In the manner of the late nineteenth-century Turkish sultan, Abdul Hamid II, Qadhafi is preoccupied with his own security. He moves restlessly from residence to residence to avoid providing opportunity for assassins. When he flies, all other airplanes in Libya are usually grounded. He is also adept at

moving back from the brink of destruction just when he has almost incited his adversary to attack him, a response frequently evident in Qadhafi's confrontations with Egypt. In 1981, when the U.S. Navy responded to his provocations by shooting down two Libyan aircraft, Qadhafi (who had learned of the impending naval operations several days in advance) was not even in the country.

2. Despite his well-developed instinct for survival, the desire for confrontation seems likewise to be a critical part of Qadhafi's psychological makeup. In his confrontations with enemies and those he sees as obstacles to the attainment of his goals, Qadhafi assures himself of his worthiness and receives the attention and recognition he craves. The Libyan colonel appears to enjoy accusing others of that which he is himself accused and of seeking to turn around the tactics of his perceived tormenters. For example, in an interview on Austrian television in 1984, he described President Reagan's policies as "childish" and accused Libyan dissidents in exile, several of whom had recently been assassinated by his operatives in Europe, of being the true "terrorists."

It is significant that as Qadhafi has entered middle life, with the attainment of his goals still almost as remote as when he first came to power, he has begun to engage in ever more flamboyant acts of international lawlessness. His impatience appears to be growing, as, most likely, will his desire for confrontation. There is persuasive evidence, for example, that Qadhafi was behind the mid-1984 mining of the Red Sea and the Gulf of Suez, and that in late 1985 Libya was involved in the terrorist attacks in Europe carried out by Abu Nidal operatives (see Chapter 5). The April 1986 Libyan bomb attack on a Berlin discotheque frequented by U.S. servicemen represented a dangerous new trend, as it violated Qadhafi's usual tactic in recent years of seeking to avoid the dangers of reprisal inherent in direct targeting of Americans.

3. The psychological complexity of Qadhafi's character appears to indicate that his need for acceptance, both personal and international, arises not from feelings of inferiority but from a belief in his own superiority and his anger at the failure of others to recognize it. Through his own behavior, Qadhafi has

frequently realized his worst fears of retaliation. According to some observers, even his own aides avoid pushing Qadhafi into a corner, where he might "seek the satisfaction of martyrdom." This assessment appears to corroborate the suspicion that Qadhafi would, like a troublesome child, rather be punished than ignored.

Nonetheless, because he was apparently looked down upon as a child for his Berber heritage, Qadhafi is probably also motivated by a desire to be accepted as a pure or even as "the truest" Arab. This drive, and a parallel rejection of Western materialist culture, has given him a puritanical bent—hence his indulgence in such curiosities as a personal aircraft in which the seats have been removed so that passengers may recline on Arab-style cushions for the journey. At the same time, his sense of drama has also promoted a hybrid life-style involving colorful capes, flamboyant uniforms, and female bodyguards.

4. Even beyond the need for acceptance, the need for recognition—the drive to be on center stage—infuses Qadhafi's behavior. His grandiose self-assessment allows him to define himself as an opposition figure on a worldwide scale. The fact that he is usually held at arm's length by other heads of state—including those whose admiration he desires, such as the Ayatollah Khomeini—appears to have reinforced his dedication to his mission as well as his perception of himself as a "chosen" person.

5. The messianic vision that feeds his fervor as well as his sense of importance makes Qadhafi a fascinating psychological study. Instead of being unpredictable, however, he is more often than not highly regular in his responses. Nonetheless, his two deepest psychological drives—the fear of failure and a determination for revenge—typically move him to commit actions that appear contradictory. While offering to improve diplomatic relations with a given country, for example, he frequently increases subversive efforts against that country. This is not a new international phenomenon, of course. But one reason for the frequent criticism leveled at Qadhafi for using this paradoxical procedure is the bumbling behavior of Libyan operatives, which often brings Libyan covert activities into public view.

Efforts by Westerners to define Qadhafi's psychological state frequently result in the judgment that he is mad. But his acts must be judged in the context of his society as well as of his background. Any Western leader who drew a revolver and fired repeatedly into the ceiling to express his emotions would almost certainly be removed quickly from office. The fact that Qadhafi has occasionally resorted to such behavior may merely underscore his willingness to express his exuberance or his sorrow in a typically Arab manner. (Of course, most Arabs who fire in the air to express excitement prefer to do so outside.) But firing a weapon probably also reflects Qadhafi's shrewdness in manipulating the considerable macho conditioning of his followers.

6. Qadhafi grew up in a household of women, and women have clearly had a strong influence on him. He was reportedly close to his mother, who died in the late 1970s. The phenomenon of male adulation in Arab culture, reinforced by the circumstances of Qadhafi's upbringing, point to his strong need to surround himself with adoring and strong but subordinate women. The traditional values set forth in the "Green Book" relegate women to a secondary role in life, although Qadhafi seeks to define that role as separate but equal. Libya's sparse population and the need to employ womanpower as well as manpower toward achievement of his goals have certainly prompted Qadhafi to advance such ultimately liberating policies as military service for women.

Qadhafi's relationships with women are one aspect of his private life that he guards jealously. Only a few such details are ever made public. He was married briefly to Fathia Khalid, the daughter of the Fezzen security service head, Brigadier Nuri Khalid. The marriage produced one child and ended in divorce in 1970, the year he married his present wife, Safiya. A nurse by profession, Safiya is from the Bara'sa tribe in Cyrenaica. She has borne three children to Qadhafi and is said to hold his respect for her intelligence. On occasion she accompanies her husband on official missions, as she did in late 1985 on a trip through West Africa. But she usually remains very much in the background.

Qadhafi's reputation for "purity" has seldom been questioned. Unlike others of the Free Officers group, he was neither a drinker nor a womanizer in his youth. On the other hand, although rumors in recent years of his liaisons with young women in his entourage and even of his efforts to seduce foreign visitors are not well documented, some accounts do have the ring of truth. Still, Arab culture would not generally condemn promiscuous behavior by a male; if anything, it would be somewhat inclined to consider sexual advances as evidence of virility and as a natural reaction to the presence of a female.

7. Qadhafi's goals are clear: He seeks to create an Islamic bloc based on the Third Universal Theory, as outlined in his "Green Book." Libya, where the theory will first be applied, will serve as a model to the rest of the Arab, African, and nonaligned worlds. In the course of this creation, Qadhafi intends to punish the West for past transgressions against the Arabs and to restore the Arabs to the international preeminence that is the rightful position of the followers of the religion of God. Destruction of the state of Israel is a necessary precursor to the return of usurped Arab lands and the vindication of offended Arab honor. Ultimately, international acceptance of the Third Universal Theory will entail rejection of both capitalism and communism.

The obstacles to achievement of these goals are formidable, as Qadhafi is well aware. In recent years he has thus directed his attention to the issue of eliminating those who impede his progress: the Libyan dissidents, the moderate Arabs, and the United States. The dissidents, both at home and abroad, are his primary targets and the obstacle against which the majority of his energy is directed.

EVOLUTION OF TACTICS

In the years since 1969 Qadhafi's goals have not changed, nor have his tactics been conspicuously altered. The man has, however, become more calculating, more ruthless, and somewhat more effective in his ability to press for advantage and for the fulfillment of his objectives. Yet Qadhafi is basically an opportunist who, like water, flows in where there is an opening. He seeks center stage—the world's attention—and will have it even if, to get it, he must indulge in behavior most of the rest of the world considers outrageous or contemptible.

Qadhafi's preferred political tactics are of the classic carrot-and-stick variety: He frequently offers blandishments such as financial aid or even political unity while, at the same time, working through covert means or threats to bend his target to his will. His efforts to destabilize those who oppose him or are regarded as friends of the West are consistent with his desire for a new world order, the achievement of which he has on several occasions advocated through "world revolution." Qadhafi is not, however, insensitive to the fact that his tactics frequently violate accepted norms of international behavior, and he fiercely denies accusations that he supports or engages in terrorism. By opening the possibility of using Abu Nidal operatives, he can hope to hide his involvement in specific operations and increase his impact. The extent to which Abu Nidal will consent to being used by Libya is not yet clear, however.

In the years since the revolution, Qadhafi's relationship with those who came to power with him has radically changed. Only a few of the original Free Officers group survive politically, and even they are subject to suspicion and demotion. Ever-present security forces watch the activities even of those within the inner circle. The military, identified at the time of the revolution as being "one with the people," had by the early 1980s become a source of growing irritation to Qadhafi. In 1982 he began publicly to criticize his military officers as a parasitic lot with no part in "the people."

The radical switch in Qadhafi's regard for the military is only one of several changes that have come over him in the years since 1969. His fanaticism, his inflexibility, and his self-righteousness have deepened. Subject to swings of mood and periods of depression that result in retreats from public life, sometimes for weeks at a time, Qadhafi has failed to mellow with age. As he has entered midlife and reviewed his progress toward achieving his goals, his impatience has increased. The series of flamboyant acts of international terrorism carried out by Qadhafi's operatives beginning in 1984 reflect not only his desire to punish those who oppose him but also his need to be on center stage and his impatience with the slow fruition of his goals.

Under pressure, particularly military pressure, Qadhafi is nevertheless capable of retreat. When threatened with retaliation he can abort his plans, as, for example, he has occasionally done when advised that actions planned against U.S. personnel or installations would bring U.S. counteraction. But these retreats are temporary and calculated: Qadhafi searches for new opportunities, but he does not change his goals. Moreover, the most effective threats against Qadhafi appear to be private threats that avoid publicly humiliating him. For several years Algeria and Egypt have pushed back at Qadhafi in this manner (albeit with limited success), responding to his posturing and plans with private communications that allow him to understand that retaliation will follow swiftly if he does not back off from specific activities. Obviously, such methods of countering Qadhafi are not available to his weaker neighbors or to the Libyan people themselves. In both quarters he has responded with increasing heavy-handedness.

Spiritual decay sometimes comes to visionaries for whom fulfillment is too long delayed. And, indeed, one symptom of Qadhafi's decay has been his resort to retribution—uncharacteristic of his youth but now apparently self-excused as he lashes out at those he sees as his betrayers. Executions for economic and political crimes were virtually unknown in Libya in the first six or seven years after Qadhafi came to power. Nor in the early years did he actively threaten his weaker neighbors, with the exception of Chad, a part of which he annexed in 1973. In October 1980, however, the Libyans mounted a major invasion of Chad, and in 1981 Qadhafi warned Niger that it could be next after Chad to receive his attention. At the time of this writing (Spring 1986), Libya's bullying of Tunisia remains a source of serious regional tension.

QADHAFI'S IDEOLOGY

As noted, Qadhafi issued in 1972 what he called the Third Universal Theory—a simplistic historical and social philosophy that he has since codified in the "Green Book." Divided into three parts, this document details "The Solution of the Problem of Democracy" (1976), "The Solution of the Economic Problem"

(1978), and, finally, "The Social Basis of the Third Universal Theory" (1979). In it Qadhafi provides a quaint, sometimes radical, sometimes iconoclastic worldview that deals in absolutes and sets forth an uncompromising position, which thus far he has not successfully been able to implement even in Libya itself. But what Qadhafi purports to do in the "Green Book" is to prescribe "the comprehensive solution of the problems of human society so that the individual may be materially and spiritually liberated . . . a final liberation to attain his happiness."

Basically, that is, the "Green Book" seeks to explain the structure of the ideal society (Parts 1 and 2) and the evolution of history (Part 3). Qadhafi rejects communism and capitalism as well as all other previous attempts to achieve democracy, confidently declaring on the first page of Part 1 that his work contains "the final solution to the problem of the instrument of governing." The basic problem of society, in Qadhafi's view, is conflict between various groups, be they tribes, classes, parties, or other interest groups. But majority rule is unfair to the minority, he claims. Both parliaments and political parties are undemocratic because "representation is a falsification of democracy." Even plebiscites are "a fraud against democracy." Nonetheless, Qadhafi insists, a way has been found to provide for direct democracy and rule by the people, not by their representatives.

According to Qadhafi's theory of direct democracy, "popular congresses are the only means to achieve popular democracy. Any system of government other than popular congresses is undemocratic." His efforts to deliver authority to the people, to provide for "supervision of the people by the people," offer little clear direction on how to proceed other than through self-supervision and reliance on "the natural law," which all societies have developed based on their particular traditions and religion. "The natural law of any society is either tradition (custom) or religion. Any other attempt to draft law from any society outside these two sources, is invalid and illogical," according to "The Solution of the Problem of Democracy." This natural law, in Qadhafi's system, clearly indicates the need for "popular congresses and popular committees everywhere" by which "society is its own supervisor." The entity thus governed is described by Qadhafi as a *Jamahiriyya*, a coined word meaning "state of the masses."

Unlike most other authoritarian leaders, Qadhafi has sought to encourage popular participation in government. But this willingness to interact with popular opinion, in combination with his belief that he personally knows the "truth," has created a very difficult and ambiguous situation for all concerned. On the one hand, Qadhafi calls on his people to take charge of their lives; on the other, he harangues them for their mistakes. In short, while promising to act only according to the will of the people, he goads the Libyans to become different from what they are.

Inherent in the "Green Book" is the slogan under which the Free Officers came to power: "Freedom, Socialism, and Unity." The Third Universal Theory purports to show the way to freedom from economic want and from foreign as well as domestic oppression; the way to socialism, meaning social justice; and the way to unity, which to Qadhafi means first Arab unity and then unity of all Muslims, followed by (and here the picture begins to grow hazy) unity of all Third World people against those who oppress them. Although not particularly inflammatory in tone, the work is clearly revolutionary in intent. Its objective is to prompt oppressed people the world over to throw off their oppressors and seize power themselves. "Man's freedom is lacking if someone else controls what he needs," Qadhafi writes. And this must not be allowed to continue, for "In need, freedom is latent"—a quotation often seen on billboards in Tripoli.

Nor is this need for freedom limited to individual or national freedom. Qadhafi's rejection of both communist and capitalist systems as oppressing and exploiting the developing world is reminiscent of China's Theory of the Three Worlds, which also advocated cooperation among exploited Third World countries to counter the superpowers. Finally, the Third International Theory is also reminiscent, in focus at least, of another interpretation of international relations: the North-South phraseology that pits the "have nots" of the developing world against the "haves" of the industrialized states.

Qadhafi's theory holds that nationalism and religion are the two main propelling forces of history. The nation, which is composed of families and tribes, is the largest possible cohesive group: Loyalty to a larger group is beyond the comprehension or ability of individuals. History is a cyclical process of conquest, expansion, and redivision as nations assimilate one another and empires rise and fall. The necessary thing, then, is to get off this wheel of history, to find a means to subsist within the national unit. Qadhafi's answer in the "Green Book" is simple: "There is no other solution but to be in harmony with the natural rule that each nation has one religion. When the social factor is compatible with the religious factor, harmony is achieved and the life of groups becomes stable and strong and develops soundly."

Qadhafi draws a line between the nation and the state, with the latter considered "an artificial economic and political system, sometimes a military system." Libya is a state, but its real identity is as a part of the Arab nation—hence Qadhafi's nearly constant efforts to achieve political union between Libya and other Arab states. The Arab world from the Fertile Crescent to the Maghrib is for Qadhafi a single unit, and its division into separate states constitutes one of the great tragedies of history—a triumph for the imperialists who desire to divide and conquer.

Qadhafi's effort to discover an ideal or utopian society, despite his recognition of the central importance of religion to national identity, pertains to the here and now and displays no concern with an afterlife. Islam is not mentioned in the "Green Book," but religion is discussed as a primary source of moral suasion and natural law. Nonetheless, as G. E. von Grunebaum has pointed out, the quest for the correct life is the supreme motive of the Islamic experiment:[4] Qadhafi is only one of the most recent in a long list of Muslim idealists who have sought the Golden Age. If Qadhafi had lived in another generation, he might have been a prophet rather than a ruler.

The absolutes contained in the "Green Book" range in a rather naive manner from the theoretical to the biological, thus detracting from Qadhafi's argument as much as they display his breadth of interest. He rambles from topic to topic, expounding on subjects that interest him and, to his mind, provide examples to prove his basic thesis. In his black and white world

of absolutes, Qadhafi speaks concretely of the innate differences
between men and women, differences that dictate that "man
and woman cannot be equal" although "man and woman are
equal as human beings." Women suffer from "the three fee-
blenesses" of menstruation, pregnancy, and lactation, and con-
fusion has resulted from the failure to allow women the freedom
to maintain their role. In a similar vein, Qadhafi holds that
social preferences are carried in "cells" and "genes" and "trans-
mitted by inheritance." He believes, furthermore, that "blacks
will prevail in the world" because they are motivated to "ven-
geance and domination" by the discrimination and exploitation
they have suffered—this despite the fact that blacks "are sluggish
in a climate that is always hot."

Of particular interest are Qadhafi's economic theories. In
brief, a worker is a slave because he exchanges his labor for a
wage. Society's resources, moreover, are exhaustible and limited
and thus in need of equitable distribution. The answer to this
dilemma is that the producer must become the consumer, "to
abolish wages, free man from slavery to them, and return to
the natural laws that prevailed before the appearance of classes,
man-made governments, and artificial laws." Under such a
system, the motivating force becomes not profit but satisfaction
of the individual through fulfillment of his or her basic needs.

These needs are four: a place to live, an income, means
of transportation and—an interesting conclusion for a man from
a nomadic background—land. The practical implementations of
this system of "partners, not wage earners" include the following:
No person in Libya may own a house that he rents to another;
the amounts allowed in savings accounts must be strictly limited;
and land, although it is a commodity that may be used and
even bequeathed to heirs, can never be personally owned in a
legal sense. (In late 1985 zealous revolutionary committee members confiscated and burned land records in a show of enthusiasm
for Qadhafi's rejection of the principle of private ownership.)
Qadhafi foresees a time when money will be abolished, possibly
in exchange for a barter system under which each individual
will produce according to his or her needs and all will be
satisfied.

The ideology that guides Qadhafi's foreign policies must be extrapolated from the social, historical, and economic theories expounded in the "Green Book." Essentially, Qadhafi's belief in the moral righteousness of his cause, bolstered by his conviction of the correctness of his theories, gives him license to engage in an aggressive foreign policy. If his neighboring governments will not listen to reason, he is justified in working to destabilize them so as to set their people free to build a society based on the Third Universal Theory. And if his fellow Arabs do not respond to his calls for unity, it becomes his duty to seek the higher good of the Arab nation by working—through terrorist means if necessary—to move forward to the day when Arab unity can be achieved. For Qadhafi, the end clearly justifies the means.

NOTES

1. According to some accounts, Qadhafi is actually several years older than he claims to be. (See, for example, Lisa Anderson, in *Voices of Resurgent Islam*, p. 139.) His father, Abu Minyar al-Qadhafi, was said by the official Libyan news agency, JANA, to have been 100 when he died in early 1985. That number, however, seems to be a round figure denoting considerable age, the exact calculation of which is not important in bedouin culture.

2. Mohamed Heikal, *The Road to Ramadan*, pp. 70–71.

3. Oriana Fallaci, "The Iranians Are Our Brothers: An Interview with Colonel Muammar el-Qaddafi of Libya."

4. G. E. von Grunebaum, *Islam: Essays in the Nature and Growth of a Cultural Tradition*, p. 4.

4
Internal Political Dynamics

The Libyan people have experienced many direct benefits as a result of the 1969 revolution. Libya's national wealth and international influence have soared, and its national standard of living has risen dramatically. There are virtually no beggars or homeless persons in Libya's two large cities, Tripoli and Banghazi—a reflection of the more equitable distribution of wealth there than in some other developing, petroleum-rich states. Moreover, the system of "basic people's congresses" has created an expanded popular political role. Since 1969 educational and professional opportunities for women have improved, infant mortality has dropped to the internationally respectable level of approximately 82 per 1,000 live births, and significant government investments have been made in roads, ports, airports, and communications systems. Moreover, between 1971 and 1984 the average life expectancy increased from 52 to 58 years.

Nonetheless, the Libyan revolution has not been a domestic success. Qadhafi and his Free Officers have been unable to achieve their primary objective of engendering a revolutionary spirit in the Libyan people, many of whom continue to resent being coerced into participating in the political process. In the years since Qadhafi assumed control, his efforts to involve the Libyan people in running their country have included the 1973 Cultural Revolution, announcement of "people's power" in 1975, establishment of Libya as a "state of the masses" in 1977, and dramatic reduction of the power of the basic people's congresses in favor of the Revolutionary Committee system during the

63

early 1980s. It is a paradox that despite these efforts and the fact that the Socialist People's Libyan Arab Jamahiriyya is described as a "popular democracy," final authority remains in the hands of Qadhafi alone.

The result of the Libyan political experiment has been a steady progression toward greater authoritarianism as all alternate authority bases have been undercut and the more moderate voices in Qadhafi's inner circle have been gradually eliminated. When "the people" and Qadhafi disagree, Qadhafi—who considers himself one of the people but with more insight than others—casts his veto. In his view, lack of popular agreement with his positions illustrates lack of revolutionary conviction, a problem that must be corrected through "guided democracy." Both internal discontent and external opposition to Qadhafi's rule have mounted in recent years. Although the military remains the only direct threat to Qadhafi's tenure—other than that posed by the hypothetical lone gunman willing to die in an assassination attempt—serious economic difficulties beginning in 1981 have heightened tensions within both the government and the military and could eventually threaten Qadhafi's position.

GOVERNMENT STRUCTURE: THEORY AND PRACTICE

Libya is divided into several military districts or governorates (the number fluctuates between seven and ten) in which direct central control is asserted through complex and overlapping military and security organizations. Each of the twenty-five or so municipalities, which operate at the next lower administrative level, contains several districts that, in turn, are divided into villages or urban wards—the level at which the basic people's congresses operate.

In a *Jamahiriyya*, as Qadhafi envisions it, a parallel system of government is theoretically intended to extend authority from the basic to the national level through a system of people's organizations. Administrative affairs are the responsibility of the basic people's committees and, on a higher level, the municipal people's committees, which are both geographically and functionally based. Membership in these committees is more or less determined by central authority. Political affairs come under the authority of the parallel basic people's congresses, in which membership is determined by residence and for which meetings are scheduled thrice yearly. As originally set up in the late 1970s, a Congress Guidance Committee drafts resolutions to be acted upon, chooses members of the municipal people's committees, and serves as a liaison with the General People's Congress (GPC) at the national level. In 1984 the number of basic people's congresses expanded dramatically as the regime sought to control opposition to its policies by organizing its supporters among "the people." In May 1985 there were reported to be 2,236 functioning basic people's congresses.

Both the municipal people's committees and the basic people's committees, as well as the basic people's congresses, send delegates to the General People's Congress. The GPC functions as a parliament, meeting once or twice a year to implement as national policy the decisions of the popular committees. Attended by well over a thousand delegates, the GPC is both an executive and a legislative body. It is headed by a General Secretariat (which the people's congresses theoretically control) and is said to have authority over several General People's Committees each of which is headed by a secretary with cabinet-level authority.

In November 1977, in an effort to encourage direct participation of the masses in government, Qadhafi introduced the first revolutionary committees (RC). These nonofficial popular watchdog organizations further complicate an already intricate system. Their main function appears to be encouragement of the people to establish people's congresses in order to struggle against the bureaucracy of the people's committees—and then to create additional revolutionary committees. RCs also send delegates to the General People's Congress, where they have become increasingly powerful; but they have assumed a vigilante role, as well—a role that during the past few years especially has heightened government infighting and contributed to controversy, fear, and stalemate in the bureaucracy. Given authority by Qadhafi in 1979 to organize basic people's congress elections, the revolutionary committees have, in effect, the power to select delegates to the General People's Congress.

Although the revolutionary committee system was also extended to the military in 1979, its access to authority in that sphere continues to be limited by the self-protecting military establishment.[1] Extension of revolutionary committees to the court system has been more successful from the regime's standpoint. Beginning in 1981, revolutionary committee members were encouraged to conduct public "corruption trials" of those individuals they considered guilty of crimes against the revolution. The revolutionary courts have no formal appeals procedure, and defendants may be tried *in camera* and with no legal representation.

Citizens have not only the right but the obligation to join any and all people's groups that fall within their areas of residence, occupation, or responsibility. The sole exceptions appear to be the banks and the Libyan petroleum industry, which have generally remained exempt from intrusion by people's committees, people's congresses, and revolutionary committees. This exemption is a phenomenon that reflects Qadhafi's concern to avoid popular interference with the country's economic lifeline. In other areas of the economy not spared the assistance of popular expertise and opinion, the negative impact on administration and production has often been considerable.

In practice, the Libyan system of government works neither smoothly nor to the apparent satisfaction of either Qadhafi or the Libyan people. The traditional Libyan suspicion of government is still evident, and most Libyans are not as eager to participate in "direct democracy" as Qadhafi has wished. Attendance at basic people's congresses must frequently be enforced, and many members show up unfamiliar with the issues to be discussed. Moreover, despite Qadhafi's attempts to overcome the traditional sentiments of his countrymen, there was only one woman delegate to the General People's Congress in late 1984. In an April 1985 speech, Qadhafi severely criticized the people's congresses, exhorting members to be enthusiastic, revolutionary, and honest, and warning that those who fail "will be taken to task" and that "there will be no mercy." In other speeches Qadhafi has revealed his perception of a growing abuse of power by basic people's committee and revolutionary committee members and of the basic people's committees' failure to take leadership responsibility seriously.

This latter problem has been created in part by the increasing power of the revolutionary committees, which have special access to Qadhafi and the members of which continue a process of encroachment on the authority of the more broadly based and generally less ideological people's committees. According to *Africa Confidential*, Qadhafi "has skillfully managed to establish an extra-legal body of 'shock troops of the Libyan revolution' in his 'revolutionary committees.'"[2] Violent confrontations have occasionally occurred between the "official" people's groups and the revolutionary committee members.

Qadhafi has no formal position within Libya's loose government structure, preferring instead to demonstrate the rulership of the people by standing back from official office. Nonetheless, his power over the GPC—and thus over the entire political process—is clear. When on occasion the GPC has defied him, he has successfully forced it to his will, as illustrated by events in early 1984. Meeting in January-February 1984, the seventh session of the GPC rejected proposals, which Qadhafi favored, to (1) abolish elementary schools in favor of parental tutoring at home; (2) introduce compulsory universal military training (a measure aimed at inducting females into the service in greater numbers); (3) revise Islamic laws giving women the same rights as men in divorce and remarriage; and (4) reduce the number of municipalities to the number of military districts (apparently in an effort to reduce local autonomy).

Qadhafi's response was swift. He publicly denounced the lack of revolutionary zeal on the part of certain "reactionary forces" and by March had organized "popular demonstrations" demanding implementation of the rejected proposals. A special session of the GPC quickly approved compulsory military training for all students, and by the end of 1984 the official media was claiming that the "Militarization of the People Law" had been approved by the basic people's congresses and by students' and women's congresses at their first sessions in 1984. Meanwhile, although efforts to abolish formal elementary education were shelved, at least some measures geared toward implementation of Qadhafi's wishes regarding elementary education moved forward.

QUALITY OF LIFE

To an increasing degree, Libya is a country in which the majority of citizens live in a climate of suspicion and mistrust. Since 1981, especially, two factors have combined to decrease the quality of life in Libya: a deteriorating economy, and Qadhafi's enhanced feelings of insecurity and dissatisfaction with the progress of the revolution.

Despite a program in which basic commodities are subsidized, prices doubled in 1984 and since then have continued to climb steeply. Visitors to Libya report severe shortages of consumer goods, including fresh foods, in major cities. A system of state-run supermarkets has aroused public resentment and made these poorly stocked government stores targets for vandalism and, occasionally, even for attack by political dissidents. A rationing system was set up in late 1984 to regulate supplies of commodities such as cars, furniture, appliances, and food, but the growing black market has become a source of official concern. Farmers frequently refuse to deliver their produce to the government for resale in state stores, selling it themselves at higher prices on the black market.

Although construction of public housing continues, supply shortages and a lack of trained carpenters have turned the repair of existing buildings into a constant problem. Public services, including transportation systems, have deteriorated under economic austerity programs. Although the country's economic and social-welfare institutions are already suffering from lack of trained personnel (as well as lack of funds and a surplus of government interference), in recent years the Libyan government has sought, at times through radical measures, to cut down on expensive foreign expertise. In a January 1985 speech, Qadhafi called for elimination of "a huge army" of foreign teachers as well as of the thousands of foreigners involved in construction, advocating instead an interchange of professions and skills by Libyans themselves and organization of "the Jamahari suburb," a concept of utopian self-reliance. But the expulsion during 1984 and 1985 of some 60,000–70,000 guest workers who performed services such as garbage collection, hair dressing, baking, and domestic chores has created difficulties ranging from health hazards to bread shortages. (Approximately 200,000–250,000 alien workers continue to reside in Libya.)

Changes in the political climate are of somewhat less concern to many Libyans, as direct physical oppression touches the lives of only a few. But almost all Libyans were affected during the early 1980s by stricter controls on educational opportunity, travel, and business contacts abroad, and domestic resentment and malaise over the growing excesses of the revolutionary committees have increased. Feelings of insecurity experienced by Libyans abroad have fluctuated with the intensity of Qadhafi's campaigns against "stray dogs" (the euphemism used by the Libyan media to refer to exiled dissidents). During recent years, as political constraints have gradually tightened, Libyan families have frequently counseled their members abroad not to return home.

Although Libya enjoys universal adult suffrage and political authority theoretically rests with the masses, political activism is illegal except in support of government policies. The U.S. Department of State Human Rights Report for 1985 concluded that several thousand political prisoners may be held in Libya; it also pointed out that the system of justice in Libya was further diluted by a 1981 law that prohibits private law practice, making all attorneys employees of the Secretariat of Justice. In 1981 the revolutionary committees, through their parallel court system, reinstated public lashings for minor crimes. Following public hangings of students in early 1984, Amnesty International expressed alarm over conditions in Libya and urged the Libyan government to renounce its policy of "physical liquidation" of its "enemies." In mid-1984, however, the Libyan government announced the creation of "suicide squads" meant to combat dissidents at home and abroad. Reports of torture and of failure of due process are frequent: Televised accounts of trials have occasionally revealed the telltale marks of injury on the hands and faces of defendants.

Internal Security

An abortive coup attempt on May 8, 1984, mounted by Libyan exile opponents of Qadhafi but with at least some internal support, was the most publicized act of resistance since the revolution. Although the attempt revealed the continuing ineffectiveness of Qadhafi's opponents, it also served as a prelude to a short-lived reign of terror in which Qadhafi used revolutionary committee members to purge the country, including the military and the official government structure, of suspected counterrevolutionaries.

The coup attempt itself was quite simple, involving a commando attack on Qadhafi's headquarters at the Bab Azziziya military barracks in Tripoli. The Libyan National Salvation Front (LNSF), which claimed credit for the attempt, apparently trained its operatives in Sudan and infiltrated them from Tunisia. Betrayal of the operation before all personnel were in position led to a shoot-out between the infiltrators and the authorities in which the LNSF suffered a significant setback through the loss of several of its most qualified operatives. A police sweep operation followed, culminating in thousands of arrests and the execution—sometimes by public hanging—of more than a hundred suspected persons, many of whom had had no clear involvement with the dissident action.

The May coup attempt provided the young radicals in government with an opportunity to further reduce the authority of the remaining "old guard," including the original members of the Revolutionary Command Council. Although no prominent government officials or military officers were implicated, as usual the eye of suspicion was turned on the military. Major Abdel Salem Jalloud (who is apparently devoted to Qadhafi but has frequently been reprimanded by him because of Jalloud's weaknesses for women and drink) retained his position as a close adviser to the Libyan leader—certainly owing, at least in part, to his continued willingness to function as a mouthpiece for Qadhafi's revolutionary theories. The only other original member of the Revolutionary Command Council to retain a significant position in the Libyan power hierarchy, Colonel Khawaldi al-Hamaidi, became the new chief of general staff as well as commander of the revolutionary committee "shock force" tasked with suppressing political opposition.

But two other original RCC members were demoted: Army Chief of Staff General Mustapha al-Kharoubi became inspector general of the armed forces, and Brigadier Abu Bakr Yunis Jabir was temporarily removed as commander-in-chief of the armed forces. Another long-time Qadhafi associate, Colonel Yunis Bilqasim, was removed from his position as head of intelligence operations and placed in a relatively powerless position as secretary of foreign security. However, demotion—and later reinstatement—of Qadhafi's close associates, including the few remaining original Free Officers, is not an unusual occurrence. Even Jalloud has periodically been placed under house arrest as a result of Qadhafi's suspicions. In early 1986 several members of the inner circle, including Qadhafi's cousins the Qadafaadam brothers, were reported to be at least temporarily out of favor.

Radicals in Command

By early 1984 the young radical elite that both arose from and controls the revolutionary committee system appeared to have significantly increased its power against the moderate, and largely older, group of Qadhafi's advisers. The most significant legacy of the May 1984 coup attempt has, in fact, been the degree of opportunity it has provided for radical elements within Libya. These "young Turks" have Qadhafi's ear and cater to his concerns about his internal and external opponents.[3] Qadhafi in turn uses the radicals to attack his opponents but keeps their power in check by playing one faction against another.

Aware of the potential danger posed by any Libyan group that accedes to a position of power, Qadhafi has publicly criticized even the revolutionary committees for their corruption, power grabbing, and prevarication in implementing his directives. He is apparently also concerned about the possibility of cooperation among the revolutionary committees and thus seeks to control their lateral contacts. One problem posed by the radicals is their inclination to overreact to Qadhafi's directives. In early 1984, for example, zealous committee members had to be restrained from confiscating and burning automobiles in reaction to a statement by Qadhafi that symbols of bourgeois decadence should be obliterated. Nonetheless, although the radicals may at times exceed their mandate, Qadhafi is hardly in a position to criticize them for being publicly more "revolutionary" than he might deem prudent for the country's security, prosperity, or foreign relations.

Overlapping lines of authority and shadowy chains of command all leading back to Qadhafi's patronage have increased the Libyan leader's sense of security. But his basic distrust of virtually all those around him is illustrated by his ever-growing reliance on his family and tribal members to supervise his personal security as well as to command Libya's military districts.[4] Reliance on relatives has not only exposed Qadhafi to considerable amounts of incompetence and sycophancy; it has also increased the resentment of both the radical and the military elements of Libyan society and could promote the possibility of eventual cooperation against him.

Problems Within the Establishment

The growing power of the revolutionary committees is only one of several problems impeding the functioning of the Libyan bureaucracy and making daily life more difficult for most Libyans. The new elite that arose after the revolution is now seriously divided and discouraged. Moreover, Qadhafi's distrust for intellectuals makes him particularly suspicious of the bureaucracy. In early 1985, *Al-Jamahiriyya* published a document entitled "Rules for Purging Administrative Agencies, Administrative Units, and Public Companies and Installations," which revealed that violations Libyan bureaucrats can be held accountable for include, in addition to crimes against the economy, acts against "the security of the revolution" and against public morals. The lethargy that has resulted from disagreement with Qadhafi's philosophies and disappointment over the unfulfilled promises of the revolution constitute a growing problem for Libyan government personnel and for Libyan intellectuals in general.

The Military. Official distrust of the military has become accepted in Libyan life in recent years, as most of the coup attempts against Qadhafi were carried out by the military.

Qadhafi's calls for general mobilization and his efforts to implement his ideal of "people in arms" have arisen from his desire to move toward the day when a professional military—and the threat it poses to his authority—is no longer necessary. The obvious conflict between this ideal and the need for a professional army has not deterred Qadhafi. The increased power of young radicals, which he has permitted to occur in the name of people's power, has often been at the expense of vested military positions. In addition, military commanders are frequently rotated and sometimes arbitrarily demoted or retired. In the fall of 1984, for example, at least seventy senior military officers were forcibly retired. Berber officers have been a special target for demotion and rotation—a reflection of Qadhafi's fear that the Berber community could form a locus for opposition against him.

Morale problems—owing as much to inefficiency and opposition to service in Chad as to Qadhafi's loss of confidence—have been a constant feature of Libyan military life in recent years. The effort beginning in 1984 to improve military efficiency saw the gradual reorganization of the 60,000-member Libyan army along Soviet lines.[5] But the Libyan military remains capable only of small-scale combat and unconventional warfare and is not competent to carry out large-scale, sustained operations against major opponents such as Algeria or Egypt. The navy, although it is undergoing a substantial expansion program, retains a reputation as a generally ineffective force, as does the air force, which continues to rely on sizable numbers of foreign pilots, including Syrians, Pakistanis, and North Koreans, to fly its combat planes.

Despite this scenario, the members of the Libyan military live a sufficiently privileged life that their general loyalty has been ensured. Qadhafi's efforts not only to prevent military leaders from developing independent power bases but also to foment suspicions among groups of officers as a hedge against coup plotting have been generally successful. Nonetheless, fear of greater disadvantage could continue to motivate the military to seek to remove Qadhafi rather than see him fall, to its own detriment, further under the influence of the radicals.

The Technocrats. Libya's technocrats, another segment of the Libyan bureaucracy, also face serious difficulties but have less political leverage with which to defend themselves. Inefficiency and lack of expertise are growing as greater numbers of educated Libyans express their preference to live abroad. Libya's economic crisis of the early 1980s was particularly difficult for government bureaucrats and other professionals: In late 1983, according to press reports, Qadhafi reduced the salaries of civil servants at the same time that he increased those of the military forces. Corruption, an endemic problem, is another cause for concern in the civil bureaucracy. And what is perhaps even more serious for the future of the Libyan economy, the special status of exemption from political meddling previously accorded to the petroleum industry appears to be eroding as a result of Qadhafi's lowered confidence in the formal government bureaucracy and management structure.

The Merchant Class. Fear of further exploitation and confiscation of property in the name of the people is of constant concern to the decimated merchant class. Prohibitions against private enterprise, increased import restrictions, and higher taxes have taken a heavy toll on privately owned businesses in recent years, as have government regulations on the numbers of employees permitted a single firm. On more than one occasion Qadhafi has renewed his pledge "to annihilate the parasitic middle class." In 1984 and 1985 new restrictions on currency exports imposed a further hardship on merchants as well as on an even more powerless group, the approximately quarter-million alien workers. Although various trade unions exist in Libya, they all appear to be under direct government control through the Libyan General Federation for Trade Unions. These groups do not, moreover, normally concern themselves with migrant labor.

Students. Students and other intellectuals have also exhibited particular sets of problems. At present, there are approximately 8,000–10,000 Libyan students studying at colleges and universities abroad, the majority of them in Europe and the United States. Periodically the Libyan government issues orders for all students studying abroad to return home for political examination and, in some cases, punishment. April 7 is celebrated in Libya as the "cleansing of the universities," an anniversary of Qadhafi's first violent confrontation in 1975 with the country's students. Students have been hanged by the government every year since the April 1977 hanging of four students at Banghazi University on charges of sedition. Some of these executions have been public, as were the televised killings of students by their fellows (with obvious official approval) at Tripoli University in early 1984.

Farmers. The farmers of Libya are a little-noticed group, yet they, too, face considerable difficulty—as does that segment of the Libyan bureaucracy which seeks to help them. The standard of living has dramatically improved in Libya since 1969, but, at present, many Libyans continue to live in isolated communities (albeit with access to such amenities as television sets and radios), where their major occupation is subsistance farming. Adequate health and educational services have yet to be extended to some communities, and cultural obstacles to social change are strong. A major problem in several areas of the country is the falling water table, which has prompted agricultural authorities to restrict the cultivation of plants requiring high water consumption. And since its appearance in the early 1980s, a potato virus has seriously reduced that valuable cash crop.

Farming communities are now also experiencing severe shortages of supplies and equipment as a result of Libya's economic difficulties. During 1985 sporadic confiscations of items of heavy equipment, apparently by members of the revolutionary committees, resulted in the loss to individual farmers of tractors and other heavy vehicles, much of it communally used. (The reason for these confiscations is not clear, although the equipment may have been taken simply because committee members have the power to do so and know they can easily sell such valuable items.)

The primary government agencies for agricultural policy implementation are the secretariats for Agriculture and Agrarian Reform, for Dams and Water Resources, and for Land Reclamation and Development. Major agricultural projects have included irrigation systems, planting of orchards, agricultural training, mechanization, and land distribution. Most Libyan farms are very small, and the government has sought to stop further fragmentation. Yet, despite extensive government efforts since 1969 to make Libya self-sufficient in agriculture, particularly in the area of cereals such as millet, wheat, and barley, Libyan farmers produce at present less than 40 percent of the country's food requirement.

Religious Leaders. Finally, there are the religious leaders of Libya, who, like the groups mentioned previously, face continuing constraint. Qadhafi's long controversy with Libya's religious elite relates to the claim that he has, as one Egyptian observer phrased it, "played with Islam"—that is, tampered with the basics of accepted Islamic theology. But it also reflects Qadhafi's determination to disestablish a traditional rallying point for political dissent. The Libyan leader's two favorite bogeymen are the CIA and the Muslim Brotherhood—and he not infrequently accuses his internal opponents of simultaneous membership in both.

THE POLITICAL OPPOSITION

Qadhafi has revealed his awareness of the growing undercurrent of popular dissatisfaction through a gradual decrease in his contacts with the public and a considerable augmentation of personal security precautions. He maintains his office and main living quarters in a heavily guarded military compound in the Tripoli suburb of Bab Azziziya, and the focus of his attention remains on his opponents, both internal and in exile. His determination to eliminate them is reflected in an internal policy of growing repression against all voices that oppose him and in a foreign policy of export of terrorists. His opponents, however, may be benefiting from growing economic discontent in Libya and from increasing support by other Arab governments for Libyan exile groups.

Internal Opposition

At least fifteen serious assassination attempts have been made on Qadhafi since 1976, almost all conducted by the military. Periodic assaults on government installations have also occurred. A massive explosion at the Al-Abyar ammunition depot in Cyrenaica in early 1984, almost certainly the work of saboteurs, revealed Qadhafi's vulnerability despite all precautions. The coup attempt of May 1984, although it failed, was the first sign of a potentially significant operation with both internal and external support. In September 1984 another coup attempt at Misratah, apparently instigated by the military, resulted in the arrest of hundreds of military personnel and the execution of an unknown number.

Yet, although security regulations and political disinterest keep most Libyans submissive to the system, civilian discontent reveals itself through graffiti, clandestine pamphleteering, and failure to carry out government directives. Extremely little is known about dissident groups inside Libya, but anti-regime incidents appear on the whole to be spontaneous and uncoordinated. No one cause can be cited for popular opposition to Qadhafi. A list of popular grievances would include the following:

- excesses of the revolutionary committee members, including takeover of government functions at many locations and levels;
- resentment over assassination campaigns against Libyans abroad;
- nationalization practices that have caused heavy losses to private commerce and virtual elimination of the individual entrepreneur;
- restrictions on savings accounts affecting the middle and upper classes;
- restrictions on land and property ownership causing hardship to farmers and landlords as well as to ordinary citizens owning more than one dwelling;
- militarization of society, including recruitment of women into the army, massive recruitment of civil servants into the military in 1980, press ganging (i.e., forced enlistment) of young men (especially black Libyans) into service in Chad, and the January 1985 law providing for the general call-up of virtually all able-bodied Libyans between the ages of 14 and 55 (although terms of service vary, the usual requirement appears to be two days of training each month and one full month of general military training each year);

- massive arms purchases popularly believed to have created the consumer and basic-commodity shortages;
- state-run supermarkets resulting in large-scale consumer shortages; and
- military intervention in Africa, Chad in particular, which has pitted Muslim against Muslim and brought death to many young Libyans.

External Opposition

The major external centers for opposition to Qadhafi are Egypt, Iraq, the United Kingdom, the United States, France, and the Federal Republic of Germany. Although most Libyans abroad are not involved in plotting against Qadhafi, a significant percentage of them are actively opposed to him. But the Libyan exile oppositionist groups remain divided and generally ineffective. Activities are usually confined to seeking support within the exile community, and considerable energy is expended in political argument with other anti-Qadhafi groups. Most groups constitute no threat to the Libyan regime, to Qadhafi, or to Libyan officials abroad. As one analyst has noted:

> It would be an understatement to observe that the Libyan opposition is currently fragmented and without a coherent political program. With more than twenty identifiable entities, ranging from Marxist to Islamic fundamentalist to right-wing monarchist, it represents a bewildering array of forces whose sole common denominator is opposition to the regime of Muammar Qadhafi. Were these diverse groupings to coalesce in [a] common cause, Qadhafi would indeed have something to really worry about.[6]

Nonetheless, Qadhafi's opposition in exile has become more active during the 1980s. Anti-Qadhafi groups have responded to Libyan assassination campaigns against dissidents abroad by killing several official Libyans in Europe. The head of the Libyan People's Bureau in Rome was killed in January 1985, apparently in retaliation for several attacks on Libyan exiles in Italy and Greece. Moreover, official Libyans abroad now apparently face additional dangers. Because Qadhafi's policies have alienated the Shia Lebanese and some Palestinian groups, Libyan representatives abroad have also been attacked in recent years by non-Libyan Arab gunmen.

Despite official Libyan efforts to retaliate, Qadhafi's operatives remain generally incapable of reaching the major oppositionist leaders who are his primary targets. Cooperation between internal and external oppositionists may also be growing. Credit for the January 1985 assassination in Rome was claimed by Al-Burkan, a little known Libyan exile group whose name means "the volcano." This group had previously claimed several operations inside Libya and may have ties to members of the Libyan military and security services. Arab governments now supporting the exiled oppositionists can also be expected to increase pressure on various groups to consolidate their efforts.

The largest and to date most successful oppositionist group is the aforementioned Libyan National Salvation Front. Formed in October 1981, the LNSF is led by Muhammad al-Muqarief, a former Libyan ambassador. The LNSF claims that failure to formulate a regimented political program for a post-Qadhafi Libya allows it to attract anti-Qadhafi Libyans with a variety of political viewpoints. Members claim that the first order of business must be to remove Qadhafi, as "then everything else can be worked out." Although the group probably does not have more than several hundred active members, it is growing and has managed to attract major support from numerous Arab states. The LNSF claimed responsibility for the May 1984 coup attempt and organized the demonstrations that led to the April 1984 demonstration in St. James Square, London, in which a British policewoman was shot to death and several students were wounded by gunfire from the Libyan People's Bureau. A forced exodus from Sudan following Ja'afar Nimeiri's fall from power in early 1985 deprived the LNSF of its radio station and presented it with increased logistical and operational difficulties.

The Libyan National Democratic Grouping (LNDG) is an alliance formed in 1981 between two minor opposition groups. It is led by Mahmud al-Maghribi, who was Libya's first post-revolution prime minister. Although better known than some of the other groups, the LNDG may not have conducted any military operations inside Libya.

The Cairo-based Libyan Liberation Organization was formed in April 1982 by Abdul Hamid Bakkoush, a Libyan prime minister under King Idris. Bakkoush was the target of abortive Libyan assassination attempts in Cairo in late 1984 and again in late 1985. Egyptian security forces, which had penetrated the operation, turned the 1984 attempt into a sting operation involving Libyan claims to have eliminated a "traitor," who then turned out to be very much alive.

Abdel Moneim al-Huni, a former minister of the interior and minister of foreign affairs, is one of Qadhafi's most significant external opponents, owing to his extensive contacts and prestige inside Libya. Since his defection in 1976, al-Huni has not associated himself with any particular group, apparently seeing himself, instead, as a unification figure. But because he worked with Qadhafi for a number of years, al-Huni—and others like him—is tarnished in the eyes of some Libyans. An active debate continues among the exiles over the credentials of those who left Libya in 1969 and those who did not.

The Libyan students studying abroad, about half of whom are on Libyan government scholarships, are another source of opposition to Qadhafi. Most of these students are extremely circumspect both in their political contacts and in their expression of opinions, lest they come to be regarded as critical of the regime. But since 1975, Libyan students have worked both inside and outside Libya to pressure the Qadhafi regime, as illustrated once again by the student demonstrations in London in early 1984 and by the subsequent official retaliation on university campuses at home.

Despite a catalog of grievances, no groups other than the military and potentially the revolutionary committees have independent power bases that might allow them to act against Qadhafi. While individuals may privately deplore various manifestations of Qadhafi's ideology or policy, their opinions, except in unusual instances, have not been expressed in public statements or demonstrations. Moreover, tribal and religious leaders have fled the country, or have been co-opted by the regime or intimidated into silence. No individual has emerged with sufficient popular acceptance to make him a widely regarded leadership alternative. Should Qadhafi pass from the scene, either violently or peacefully, the result would most likely be a protracted power struggle in which the military would be heavily involved. That possibility alone is probably enough to prevent many Libyans from cooperating with the opposition.

NOTES

1. Nonetheless, revolutionary committees infringing on military authority is a growing problem that promises to lead to future confrontation between the two groups. Foreign journalists have reported brief armed clashes between some military units and revolutionary committee members in the aftermath of the April 1986 U.S. air raid. Outraged military personnel precipitated at least one instance of such conflict when revolutionary committee leaders—who had allocated to themselves control over anti-aircraft ammunition—were unavailable to release that ammunition in time to counter the U.S. aircraft.

2. *Africa Confidential* (London), no. 9 (April 25, 1985), p. 1.

3. One of the most ambitious of the young radicals is Musa Kusa, a leading figure in the International Revolutionary Committee (sometimes called the Libyan World Center for Resistance to Imperialism, Zionism, Racism, Reactionism, and Facism), which functions as a sort of parallel foreign ministry. Kusa has been involved in international terrorism since at least 1980—when he was expelled from Britain—and was probably involved in periodic efforts to undermine the position of Foreign Liaison Secretary Ali Turayki, widely regarded as one of Libya's more moderate and professional diplomats. Turayki was replaced in February 1986 by Kamal Hassan Mansour, the former petroleum minister. Others among the powerful new radical group are Muhammad al-Zarruq Rajab, secretary of the General People's Committee, and Ahmed Ibrahim, who is charged with running student revolutionary committees abroad. Also of considerable significance are Said Rashid, Abdullah Sanusi Rashid, and Abdullah Hijazi, all involved in "security" work both inside Libya and abroad.

4. Major figures in Qadhafi's inner circle include Khalifa Hunaysh, who controls the presidential guard as well as the "deterrent battalion," a sort of watchdog on the military, and Qadhafi's cousin, Ahmed Qadafaadam, who has the far-reaching authority to take action against "stray dogs." Other tribal members in authority are Messoud Abdel Hafid, who is in charge of the Kufra and Fezzen military

districts, and Colonel Musad Ahmad, commander of the Sirte military district.

5. The total Libyan military, including air force, navy, and army, is estimated to be about 90,000 strong. Enrollment in "popular resistance" units probably totals about 10,000 members, although these groups are planned ultimately to be much larger.

6. "The Libyan Opposition: Is It a Threat to Qaddafi?" *Focus on Libya* (Washington, D.C.: Center for International Security, July 1984).

5

Foreign Policy
of the Jamahiriyya

Libya's foreign policy is the foreign policy of one man: Mu'ammar al-Qadhafi, who eschews normal organizational procedures in favor of highly personalized government and decisionmaking. Despite the existence of several government organizations through which Libyan foreign policy is conducted, final authority in all major decisions is Qadhafi's alone. It is his ideology that fuels Libyan policy and his directives that enforce its conduct. Beyond a pragmatic switch with regard to the Soviet Union and periodic ups and downs in relations with the Arab and African states, there have been no essential changes in Libyan foreign policy since the revolution. However, the radical character of Libyan policy has become more pronounced during the early 1980s, making Libya ever more a pariah to the West and destroying much of Libya's credibility even in the Third World.[1]

The roots of Libyan policy lie in Libya's historical experience and reflect the social unrest and Nasserist philosophy that characterized the Arab world during the 1950s and 1960s. But Qadhafi has manipulated that historical experience to further his own beliefs. Central to Qadhafi's foreign policy is his perception of Libya as victim and Europe and the United States as villains. Glorying in recitals of Libya's real and alleged victimization of past and present, Qadhafi has sought to justify his own excesses, to attribute failures to others, and to incline domestic and international opinion in his favor.

83

As a rebel on a global scale, Qadhafi must keep his own anger—and, he hopes, that of the Libyan people—at a fever pitch. But as the personification of Libyan resentments, Qadhafi has contributed to the incapacitation rather than the liberation of his people. Trapped between a negative foreign policy that demands revenge upon former exploiters and socially indulgent domestic programs that provide previously unheard of benefits, the Libyan people have developed a national inertia. Qadhafi's effort during the 1980s to correct what may be a dangerous national tendency toward lack of initiative, illustrated by Libya's continuing dependence on the services and expertise of non-Libyans, is countered by his touting of Libya's victimization.

GOALS AND TACTICS

Qadhafi's foreign policy goals are a direct outgrowth of his personal ambitions and ideology (as discussed in Chapter 3). His objectives are to confound the imperialists and those he deems responsible for lack of Arab development and international power, to forge for himself a position as Arab and African leader, and to expand Libya's national frontiers so as to achieve a broader stage on which to act and more actors to implement his policies—hence his numerous offers to unite Libya with other Arab states. These goals dictate that his priority be given to the underscoring of his leadership credentials, but they also ensure that the potential subjugation of his neighbors, particularly his weaker African neighbors to the south, is of constant importance to him.

As previously noted, Qadhafi's foreign policy tools are basically of the classic carrot-and-stick variety. He offers diplomatic relations, financial assistance, and even political unity to other countries while at the same time reserving the right, either overtly or covertly, to intimidate. Resistance to his overtures and rejection of his ideology has grown more pronounced in recent years as Arabs and Africans—in addition to Western nations—have tired of his posturing and rhetoric. This resistance, combined with Qadhafi's failure to enlarge his frontiers (except through the partial occupation of Chad), has driven Qadhafi into an essentially reactive foreign policy, a policy motivated by his desire to punish those who reject him and to eliminate the obstacles to his divine mission.

Among the foreign policy tools that Qadhafi has selected are the funding and training of insurgents and dissidents from other countries; direct military intervention in other countries, as in Chad in 1973, 1980, and 1982, and Uganda in 1979; provision of safehaven for a variety of international outlaws; supply of weapons to subversives in several areas of the world, including Europe, East Asia, and Latin America as well as various African and Arab countries; the use of commercial, financial, educational, cultural, and journalistic front organizations; and destabilization, including assassination, campaigns against those national leaders who oppose him. In these ventures Libyan diplomatic facilities have served as bases for subversion and Libyan intelligence organizations as support networks for terrorist activities.

STRUCTURE OF THE LIBYAN FOREIGN POLICY ESTABLISHMENT

Libyan foreign policy is implemented through an intricate network of government organizations paralleled by private directives from Qadhafi and his inner circle. The Libyan Foreign Liaison Secretariat is ostensibly in charge of policy implementation, but in reality it is frequently circumvented by other branches of the bureaucracy. The Secretariat for External Security, the Secretariat of Justice, the divisions of General Intelligence and Military Intelligence, and the Libyan Special Security Forces all play foreign policy roles of varying importance.

Added to this more formal structure is the Revolutionary Committees Bureau—which functions as a law unto itself and sometimes seeks to undercut the efforts of more strictly official arms of the Libyan bureaucracy—and the Islamic Call Society, ostensibly an instrument for propagation of the faith but often used for political propaganda and subversion. Professional Libyan diplomats have come under intense pressure, particularly in the early 1980s, as a result of the encroachments of other government bureaus as well as of the efforts of revolutionary committee members to enhance their own positions. Revolutionary committee members may, for example, mount an assault on Libyan exiles in a foreign city without informing the diplomats at the Libyan People's Bureau as to what they are about—and then flee to leave the official personnel to bear the brunt of retaliation.

The Secretariat for External Security is a particularly important part of the foreign policy establishment. Created in February 1984 by a directive of the General People's Congress, this organization serves both a security and an intelligence-gathering function. One of its tasks is to coordinate the activities of various other intelligence and security arms, but infighting and the interjection of the revolutionary committees into the equation have made the exact functions of this secretariat somewhat hazy and open to individual interpretation. All depends on access to Qadhafi and careful attention to the question of which individuals, for the moment, have his confidence.

BACKGROUND TO THE PRESENT POLICY

Libyan foreign policy was confrontationist from the beginning—as evidenced by Qadhafi's stated decision to recover foreign bases and to oppose both communism and capitalism. The striking initial success of these goals aroused admiration in many areas of the Arab and developing worlds. By mid-1970 all British and U.S. forces had left Libya.[2] Pushing his policies of anti-Zionism, anticommunism, anticolonialism, and antiimperialism, Qadhafi became something of a champion of reawakened Arab pride, an exemplar to many young Arabs of commitment to Arab unity and of sincere and dedicated endorsement of the Palestinian cause.

Such widespread admiration was nonetheless relatively short-lived. It was not long before Qadhafi had begun to antagonize the other Arabs with his disregard for diplomatic convention and his inflexible insistence on the absolute righteousness of his own policies and philosophies. From the beginning, Qadhafi showed a particular dislike for Arab royalty. September 1970 brought the opening salvo in the now more than fifteen-year-long war of words between Libya and Jordan, for it was in that month that Qadhafi blasted King Hussein for military operations against the Palestinians. Then in 1971, and again in 1972, Qadhafi praised assassination attempts against King Hassan II of Morocco, thereby initiating an estrangement from the Arab monarch that lasted until 1984.

The seeds of Egyptian-Libyan antagonism are of interest because, in Qadhafi's view, Egypt is not only the critical linchpin to Arab unity and anti-Zionism but also the mother Arab state whose anti-Zionist and anti-Western leadership is essential. Nasser's biographer, Mohamed Husseinein Heikal, traces the origins of Egyptian-Libyan problems to Qadhafi's disapproval of Egyptian acceptance of UN Resolution 242 on Palestine and to Sadat's close association with the Soviets in the early 1970s. Qadhafi, moreover, persisted even in those days in verbally attacking Saudi Arabia's King Feisal, a close friend and financier of Egypt.[3]

A Federation of Arab Republics involving Egypt, Libya, and Syria (Sudan backed out at the last minute because of domestic unrest) was announced in April 1971. In July 1973, however, Qadhafi—chafing under Egypt's failure to move forward on the agreement—allowed an "Arab unity march" on Egypt: Some 30,000 Libyans were turned back by Egyptian security forces shortly after crossing the Egyptian border. The march occurred during the Libyan "cultural revolution," and although Qadhafi declined responsibility for the event, having temporarily resigned from all government positions, its failure was a clear setback to his unity schemes.

Egyptian-Libyan relations further declined when the Israelis shot down a Libyan airliner that had strayed over the occupied Sinai in February 1973. In April Qadhafi sought revenge for the incident by ordering an Egyptian submarine commander— under his authority by terms of the unity agreement—to torpedo the liner Queen Elizabeth II, which was en route to Israel carrying European and American Jews. To Qadhafi's chagrin, the order was quietly countermanded by Sadat. Later that year, when Egypt and Syria failed to inform him of their plans to launch the October War against Israel, Qadhafi was predictably furious. Although he gave significant financial support to Egypt as soon as the war began, Qadhafi condemned the war's objectives as too narrow (he wanted the recovery of all of Palestine) and criticized Egyptian acceptance of a cease-fire.

From that time on, Qadhafi's relations with Sadat deteriorated rapidly, leading to Libyan efforts to destabilize Egypt and a small-scale punitive military attack by Egyptian forces on Libya in 1977. Relations with Tunisia, another of Qadhafi's Arab neighbors, also turned sour. In January 1974 Qadhafi and President Habib Bourguiba signed the Gerba Agreement to merge their two countries into one Arab Islamic Republic. But this agreement was rescinded by Bourguiba almost as quickly as it had been made, leaving Qadhafi stymied once again in his desire for Arab unity.

Following the 1973 Middle East War, Qadhafi assumed a leadership position in Arab efforts to persuade black African states to break diplomatic ties with Israel. Thanks in large part to Libyan pressures, some thirty African states had done so by the end of 1973. Libyan indulgence in African adventurism also commenced at this time, including the beginning of support for oppositionist elements in Chad and the 1973 occupation of the Aozou Strip, a segment of Chad along the Libyan border. A gradual strengthening of ties with the Ugandan dictator Idi Amin, whom Qadhafi tried unsuccessfully to save from overthrow in 1979 by sending a few planeloads of Libyan troops, did nothing to enhance Libya's image in Africa.[4]

Meanwhile, Qadhafi was showing an increasing preoccupation with the possibilities of world leadership. His ideology and global aspirations were gelling, and his impatience over the lack of achievement of his domestic and international objectives was growing. Recognition of increased internal and external opposition to his leadership soon brought a pragmatic change in one of the original aspects of his foreign policy: anticommunism. In March 1972 the first high-level Libyan delegation to the USSR went to Moscow on an arms-buying mission. Within a short time, Libyan involvement in a military buildup began to drain off both funds and technical personnel. Tanks, the first Soviet arms delivery, arrived in Libya in mid-1970, but it was not until 1974 that the Soviet Union replaced France as Libya's largest arms supplier.

LIBYA AND INTERNATIONALLY OUTLAWED BEHAVIOR

Although Qadhafi denies that Libya is involved in international terrorism, Libya has armed, financed, trained, and provided safehaven to members of various terrorist, insurgent, and dissident groups since the early 1970s. Libyan efforts to destabilize moderate, pro-Western governments have been most pronounced in Africa, but in 1985 Libyan revolutionary committees and people's bureaus expanded efforts to extend their contacts into Latin America, evidently motivated by a desire both to undermine U.S. interests and to increase Libya's Third World influence. Diplomatic ties do not preclude Libyan use of clandestine methods to subvert other countries if Qadhafi decides that their leaders have strayed too far from the correct path, as demonstrated dramatically by Libya's mining of the Red Sea and the Gulf of Suez in mid-1984.[5]

As is true of Libyan relations with more legitimate groups, Libyan support for foreign subversive and terrorist organizations has vacillated. Frequently, the Libyans have not delivered promised funds or supplies, and in recent years they have angered some groups by applying greater pressure for *quid pro quo* in the form of intelligence exchange, joint operations, or greater amenability to Libyan directives. Nor has Qadhafi differentiated among genuine national liberation movements, separatist groups, commercially based terrorist outfits, and individuals with no real power base or ideology other than self-advancement. Support for clandestine organizations of whatever sort apparently appeals to Qadhafi's desire to manipulate international events.

In Europe such support has included funds (and sometimes rhetorical support) for the Provisional Irish Republican Army, the Armenian Secret Army, the Basque Separatist Movement, the Red Army Faction in West Germany, and the Popular Forces of April 25 in Portugal. Carlos Ilyich Ramirez, the well-known international terrorist of the 1970s, and members of the Bader-Meinhof gang have on various occasions received support from or found asylum in Libya. Elsewhere Libyan support has been extended to a variety of Palestinian groups including Black September and the Abu Nidal and Abu Musa factions, the Japanese Red Army, the Moro National Liberation Front in the

Philippines, and various black groups in the United States that Qadhafi hopes to stimulate into more vigorous actions against the U.S. government.

Qadhafi's sponsorship of international terrorism has taken two forms: support to non-Libyan groups, and direct use of Libyans to target his opponents—Libyan nationals as well as others—outside the country. Qadhafi's unhappiness over his rejection by the majority of the Arabs has inspired Libyan plotting and, occasionally, actual efforts to undermine or to assassinate other Arab leaders including King Hussein of Jordan, former President Nimeiri of the Sudan, and various Saudi, Egyptian, and Iraqi officials. Libyan operatives have also conducted terrorist and subversive operations in a variety of African states, including the September 1985 plot against Zaire's President Sese Seko Mobutu.

Expanded Libyan cooperation with the Abu Nidal group generated extensive Western attention and concern as a result of the terrorist attacks at the Rome and Vienna airports in late December 1985. Although the Libyans subsequently modified their initial statements of praise for the attacks, in which twenty people were killed, Tunisian authorities claimed that the suspected Abu Nidal operatives were traveling on passports that had been confiscated by Libyan authorities from expelled Tunisian workers several months earlier. The Libyans and the Abu Nidal group are likewise believed by Western intelligence sources to have been involved in the November 1985 hijacking of an Egyptian airliner to Malta, an event that resulted in the deaths of several dozen persons.

Qadhafi's preoccupation with the elimination of Libyan dissidents has direct implications for Libya's foreign relations when such attempts occur abroad. Assassination of Libyan dissidents abroad began in 1980, and only the vigilance of the targets and the ineptitude of most Libyan operatives, who are frequently "revolutionary students" fired up to work for Qadhafi, have prevented a higher death toll. In an early 1981 speech, Qadhafi proclaimed that "it is the duty of the Libyan people to constantly liquidate their opponents . . . at home and abroad, everywhere." He has publicly reiterated this sentiment on many occasions.

At least eleven Libyan opponents of Qadhafi were killed by Libyan hit teams in Europe and the Middle East in 1980 and 1981. A revival of the campaign against "stray dogs" brought a series of attacks on Libyan exiles in European cities in 1984 and 1985, resulting in at least eight more deaths. And according to the Libyan National Salvation Front, more than twenty Libyan dissidents have been killed by Libyan execution squads in Europe since early 1980.

QADHAFI AND THE BOMB

Access to nuclear technology, including nuclear weapons, appeals to Qadhafi's desire to demonstrate both Arab achievement and his own importance. Qadhafi has tried to persuade other nations—including China, Pakistan, the United States, the Soviet Union, India, France, and Argentina—to share nuclear technology with him. And he has sought assistance from at least China, Pakistan, and the Soviet Union to develop a nuclear weapons capability. Although he has not succeeded in obtaining such assistance, Qadhafi has negotiated successfully with several nations for assistance in development of civilian nuclear technology.

In 1974 Argentina agreed to train Libyan chemists in uranium extraction and purification and to provide the equipment necessary for prospecting for radioactive materials. (Uranium "yellow cake" is commercially exported by Libya's neighbor Niger, thus providing an additional reason for Libyan interest in that country.) In subsequent years Qadhafi engaged in a vigorous hiring program of nuclear scientists, sent scores of students to study nuclear technology in the West (including the United States), and established a nuclear research center at Tajura. He also sought agreements from the Soviet Union and from Belgonucleaire, a Belgium government-controlled firm, for assistance in building nuclear energy facilities.

The possibility of Libyan access to nuclear technology has from time to time caused both legitimate concern and overwrought excitement in Israel and the West. There is no indication, however, that Libya has access to the technology or resources that would enable it to construct a nuclear weapon. A key unanswered question concerns the location from which Qadhafi would obtain a reactor core—a matter no one has been willing to discuss with him. As his policies grow more eccentric and his funding more limited, access to a nuclear weapon is likely to recede even further from Qadhafi's grasp.

REGIONAL RELATIONS

Although Libya's relations with its African and Arab neighbors are of primary importance to Qadhafi, many of these ties are seriously strained. Tiny Tunisia, perched on Libya's shoulder, is particularly vulnerable, and Qadhafi has positioned his agents in that country in the hope of benefiting from the political turmoil likely to accompany the passing of aging President Bourguiba. Egypt and Algeria have grown increasingly unhappy over Qadhafi's efforts to destabilize the region and to benefit from and promote problems in Chad, Niger, and the Sudan as well as Tunisia. The mid-1984 Treaty of Oujda pledging Morocco and Libya to eventual unity was greeted with apprehension by the other North African states and has served to further polarize the region. Nonetheless, as a marriage of convenience for both parties, the Moroccan-Libyan union shows little sign of either serious deterioration or significant implementation.

Colorful invectives frequently fly between Tripoli and Cairo, and Qadhafi has warned President Hosni Mubarak that he will "meet Sadat's fate"—namely, assassination. The November 1984 Egyptian sting operation—in which Qadhafi was tricked into thinking his plans to arrange the assassination in Cairo of a former Libyan prime minister had succeeded—heightened tensions in a relationship already strained by the mid-1984 mining of the Red Sea and the Gulf of Suez. A similar Egyptian wrap-up of a Libyan effort to assassinate Qadhafi's opponents in exile occurred in late 1985. Qadhafi, however, has usually been careful not to take action where his hand is clearly revealed and as a consequence of which Egyptian retaliation would be inevitable. He cannot help but be aware that both Egypt and Algeria would like to see him removed and that, if they wish to select that option, they have their own commando forces as well as a variety of Libyan dissident organizations clamoring for assistance to do so. Moreover, both countries have regionally powerful armies of which Qadhafi is justifiably apprehensive.

Qadhafi's Arab and Muslim identity is such a critical part of his makeup that his inability to persuade the Arabs to join him in an all-out effort to eliminate Israel and to reject Western influence has been perhaps the greatest disappointment and irritant for him since the 1969 revolution. Yet, other than Morocco, only Syria, South Yemen, and Iran can be described as close Islamic world friends of Libya. But Libya has serious differences even with these states (including disagreement with Qadhafi regarding his threats to achieve Arab and Islamic unity by force). They tend to treat the mercurial Qadhafi with considerable caution, all the while seeking to harness his political support among radicals and to benefit from his financial resources.

Qadhafi's support for non-Arab Iran in its war with Iraq— a support tied to Qadhafi's admiration for militant Islam in action—has been a cause of severe criticism of Libya by most other Arab states. Likewise, the emergence of Qadhafi as a patron of the more extreme Palestinian factions and his efforts to eliminate PLO leader Yasir Arafat have had a negative impact on his relations with the other Arabs. His stationing of several hundred Libyan troops in troubled Lebanon during the late 1970s and early 1980s resulted in periodic strains in Libyan-Syrian ties but did not, as Qadhafi had hoped, enhance Libya's international position or cause the other Arabs to recognize Libya as a "front-line state" in the battle against Israel.

Qadhafi's threats and actions against the moderate Arabs have led at various times to breaks in diplomatic ties with Saudi Arabia, Egypt, Tunisia, Morocco, Iraq, and Jordan. Covert efforts by Libya in 1984 to disrupt the *hajj* (the Muslim pilgrimage to Mecca in Saudi Arabia) injected further caution into Libya's ties with several Islamic states. In recent years Qadhafi has frequently gone over the heads of the rulers to the Arab people themselves, calling on them, as he did in April 1985, to "rise and destroy the submissive traitors who have betrayed our nation."

On the southern border of Libya, Qadhafi seeks strategic domination for military as well as economic and political purposes. His objective appears to be creation of a Libyan-dominated bloc of pan-Islamic states in West Africa's Sahel region. Although he has claimed portions of the territory of all contiguous states, however, Libya is not militarily strong enough to threaten significantly any but the weakest of its neighbors. Thus Libya constitutes a strategic threat only to Chad (a portion of whose territory it continues to occupy), Niger (which Qadhafi publicly warned in 1981 would be next on his list), and Tunisia (which is weak and politically vulnerable). Libyan agents made several attempts to subvert the Nimeiri regime, but they were not involved in the successful 1985 coup. Nonetheless, the Libyans have moved quickly to position themselves for future action by moving hundreds of Libyan-trained Sudanese revolutionary committee members back into the Sudan. Despite Libyan recognition of the new Sudanese regime, continuing Libyan covert actions against the Sudan can be expected.

Farther afield, Qadhafi seeks to replace moderate African governments with regimes amenable to Libyan influence and to undercut Western, particularly French and U.S., influence. Africans in general treat Qadhafi with caution and are aware of Libya's frequent failure to live up to its financial promises. Nonetheless, Qadhafi's promises of financial benefit to those who cooperate and his threats against those who do not are powerful incentives to maintain at least cordial relations with Libya. In the mid-1980s Qadhafi continued his efforts to improve Libyan relationships with a variety of African states. But Libya's ties with Africa remained problematic. The August 1981 tripartite alliance among Libya, Ethiopia, and the People's Democratic Republic of Yemen failed to lead to effective political or military cooperation. The long close ties to Ethiopia deteriorated in the early 1980s owing in part to Libyan efforts to improve ties to Somalia. But relations with several African states remained severed, and the continued Libyan military presence in Chad, as well as the political and financial pressuring of various African governments, keeps the Africans suspicious of Libyan intentions.

FOREIGN RELATIONS

Relations with Europe

One of the central ironies of Libya's foreign policy is the country's need for close relations with those most distrusted.

Qadhafi professes to abhor the history, policies, and philosophies of the Western democracies, but he needs Western trade and technology. Despite his periodic indulgence in inflammatory anti-European rhetoric, Libya maintains extensive economic ties to the European states and desires closer relations with both eastern and western European countries as foils to both U.S.-sponsored international isolation and the need to rely totally on the Soviet Union for technology and weapons. Some 40,000 skilled workers from western Europe make a major contribution to the continued operation of Libya's economic and social systems.

Qadhafi also seeks in Western acceptance proof of his significance as an international figure. Usually held at arm's length by European leaders, Qadhafi nonetheless courts them assiduously. His impulse to seek center stage in Europe was dramatically demonstrated during the November 1985 Geneva summit between President Reagan and Soviet leader Gorbachev. Qadhafi informed the Swiss that he, too, was planning to arrive in Geneva and would lead a people's "peace march." Only an extremely sharp warning from the Swiss that he would not be allowed to enter the country deterred Qadhafi from carrying through with his plan to steal the show.

Thus, despite his desire to be accepted as an equal by the Europeans, Qadhafi frequently indulges in behavior guaranteed to alienate them. His anti-dissident operatives continue to play a game of hide and seek with western European security services, and the Libyan quest for official invitations does not preclude periodic public reminders to the Europeans that Qadhafi holds them responsible for past exploitation of Libya and is willing to hold their citizens hostage as a sign of opposition to their present policies. On several occasions in recent years, he has imprisoned Europeans, including Britons, West Germans, and Italians, in an effort to punish the captives' governments.

In an early March 1985 speech, Qadhafi again demonstrated his resentment over his European neighbors' provisions of shelter to his Libyan opponents and the European failure to turn Libyan dissidents over to him on demand. In this speech Qadhafi renewed demands to Italy for World War II reparations, adding that Britain, Germany, and "other states" must also compensate for war damage to Libya. Finally, he warned that he would deal with the Europeans on a reciprocal basis: If they support

Leonid Brezhnev greets Qadhafi as he arrives in Moscow for an official friendly visit. Photograph courtesy of UPI/Bettmann Newsphotos.

his opponents, he would "consider the Bader-Meinhof, the Red Brigades, and the IRA as revolutionary opposition." Then, following imposition of stricter U.S. economic sanctions in early 1986, Qadhafi let several European governments know that cooperation with the United States would result in Libyan-sponsored terrorist incidents on their soil.

Libya and the Soviet Union

Although Qadhafi began his leadership of Libya as an opponent of both the capitalist and the communist worlds, his political and economic struggles were with the West, thus beginning a political alienation that would eventually lead to

his present significant ties to the Soviet Union. The Libyan-
Soviet relationship is a mutually wary one in which short-term
benefits mask long-term disagreements. Despite Soviet contempt
for Libya's political maverick, who is scarcely amenable to
Moscow's directives, the benefits accruing to both parties are
sufficient to keep the relationship vigorous.

Since the signing of the first major Soviet-Libyan arms
agreement in 1974, Moscow has sold Tripoli some 15 to 20
billion dollars' worth of armaments, thus providing the Soviets
a much-valued source of hard-currency earnings. Qadhafi's
policies, moreover, keep the West on edge and contribute to
destabilization in several areas of the world from which the
Soviets can hope to benefit. For their part, the Libyans receive
not only vast quantities of modern weapons and technical
assistance but also the solicitous attention of a superpower that
Libya seeks to play off against the West. Currently working in
Libya are some 6,000 Soviet personnel, as well as at least 30,000
Eastern European and 4,000 Cuban advisers and technicians
(see Table 5.1).

Although Qadhafi refused a Soviet request for military
bases in 1979, he has occasionally warned in recent years that
he will provide the Soviets with basing privileges if the West
continues to threaten him. In the event of a major European
war, it is presumed that Qadhafi would allow the Soviets the
use of his facilities. The Soviet navy already enjoys access to
Libyan ports, and Qadhafi has permitted the Soviets to fly from
Libyan air bases in order to monitor NATO naval activities and
to use Libyan bases in air-supply operations to Africa. Yet Libya
does not function as a massive arms depot for potential Soviet
use: On the one hand, the number of Libyan pilots, technicians,
and other personnel is insufficient to operate the massive arms
purchases; on the other, less than adequate attention has been
given to maintenance and storage so that much of the supposed
stockpile has deteriorated beyond use.

Moscow seeks to avoid identification with Qadhafi's controversial activities; thus, despite the Libyan announcement in
1983 that a Soviet-Libyan Friendship and Cooperation Treaty
would be signed between the two countries, this development
has not transpired. (Libya signed Friendship and Cooperation

TABLE 5.1
Foreigners residing in Libya

American	800-1,000
Bangladeshi	6,000
British	5,000
Bulgarian	7,000-8,000
Cuban	4,000
Egyptian	110,000
Filipino	5,000
French	2,500
German (West)	1,500
Italian	12,000-15,000
Korean (South)	18,000
Moroccan	3,000
Pakistani	20,000
Polish	8,000-10,000
Romanian	15,000
Soviet	6,000
Sudanese	15,000-20,000
Syrian	20,000
Tunisian	50,000-60,000
Turkish	35,000-40,000
Yugoslavian	10,000-12,000

NOTE: The Libyan economy remains dependent on
foreign laborers as well as on foreign experts. No
accurate official statistics are available on
foreigners living in Libya, the number of whom has
fluctuated in recent years between 250,000 and
500,000. All figures are approximate and--especially
with regard to figures for Libya's fellow Islamic
states--possibly inaccurate by several thousand in
either direction. Representatives of other
nationalities not listed here also reside in Libya.

treaties with Czechoslovakia and North Korea in 1982 and with Bulgaria and Romania in 1983.) In late 1985 Qadhafi made his first trip to Moscow in several years, a visit that, by all indications, underscored deep differences between the two countries—despite the signing of agreements on economic, scientific, and technical cooperation, political consultations, and consulates. The Soviets expressed unhappiness over Qadhafi's condemnation of a negotiated peace settlement in the Middle East, as well as over his unauthorized supply of Soviet arms to Iran, his calls for the elimination of Israel, and his efforts to pressure the Soviets into greater acceptance of oil rather than currency in exchange for arms.

No basic changes can be expected in the Libyan-Soviet relationship in the near future. Qadhafi remains as opposed to communism as he ever was, but his intention is to prevent the West—through his relationship with Moscow—from retaliating against him. Moscow will continue to sell arms to Qadhafi (including SA-5 missiles in late 1985) as a source of currency, but it could encounter even greater difficulty in the form of Libyan nonpayment of its arms debt to the Soviet Union, a debt that already totals at least $7 billion.

Libya and the United States

Qadhafi sees the United States as the greatest ultimate obstacle to achievement of his political and ideological objectives.[6] He has described the United States as a country "whose mission is to dominate the world" and whose support for Israel and policies in the Third World constitute "international terrorism." In a 1984 interview with Vienna Television, Qadhafi said:

> The United States is under the influence of Zionism. Zionism is trying to destroy the American interests in the world and this Zionist policy will lead the United States into catastrophe because the American policy under the Reagan administration leads directly into a confrontation with the Soviet Union in the Middle East. We have declared many times that we want to establish good relations with the United States, but it has refused this to date. The United States wants to bring Libya under its influence, wants to enslave us, but we want to be free.

Although Qadhafi clearly feels that his tenure is being threatened by the United States, it is also apparent that his highly publicized controversy with the United States—particularly under the Reagan administration—has provided him with significant gratification. Indeed, any identification of Libya as a major opponent tends to raise Qadhafi's feelings of personal and national significance and caters to his sense of being a key player on the international scene. On numerous occasions,

Qadhafi has offered both privately and publicly to work with the United States to reduce tensions. But the U.S. government has rejected these overtures on the grounds that Qadhafi has a record of offering to negotiate as a means of deflecting attention from continuing efforts to undermine him. It is a major irony of the Libyan-U.S. relationship that Qadhafi feels a need for U.S. recognition of his importance—one indication among others, perhaps, that he admires the United States for its power, position, wealth, and technology. (The Libyan people, on the other hand, appear to have considerable admiration for American consumer goods, as well as American personal freedoms and life-styles.)

Libyan-U.S. relations in the Qadhafi era have been on a progressive downhill slide beginning with the evacuation of U.S. bases from Libya, takeovers of U.S. oil assets, and Libyan participation in the Arab oil boycott in the early 1970s. The U.S. diplomatic mission in Libya was closed in May 1980 following several years of deteriorating relations climaxed by the sacking and burning of the U.S. Embassy in late 1979. In May 1981 the Libyan diplomatic mission in Washington was closed on grounds of providing assistance to illegal and terrorist operations. And in August 1981 U.S. naval maneuvers in the Gulf of Sidra—in effect, a challenge to Libyan claims of territoriality over international waters—resulted in the shooting down of two Libyan aircraft by U.S. planes.

Unilateral U.S. economic sanctions against Libya, first instituted in 1978, have been gradually expanded. With the partial exceptions of food and drugs, virtually all U.S. exports to Libya now require a validated export license. Qadhafi continues routinely to accuse the United States of using economic as well as political means to attempt to destabilize Libya and to undermine its international position. The Libyans have carried this complaint to the United Nations and have sought but failed to obtain Third World support to move the UN headquarters out of the United States. In late 1985 Qadhafi canceled a planned appearance at the fortieth anniversary celebration of the UN, claiming that the Libyan people believed it was too dangerous for him to visit the United States.

Qadhafi's fear of U.S. retaliation has, with few exceptions, prevented him from directly targeting U.S. personnel and installations. Exceptions have included his plans to assassinate the U.S. ambassador to Egypt in 1978 and the U.S. ambassador to Italy in 1981, as well as a 1981 plan to blow up an American social club in Khartoum, Sudan. Much-publicized Libyan schemes to assassinate President Reagan in 1981 were subsequently revealed almost certainly to be bogus intelligence reports— reports that may have been the result of a deliberate misinformation campaign by a third party interested in keeping tensions high between the United States and Libya. In May 1985 the Federal Bureau of Investigation uncovered a Libyan plan to execute Libyan dissidents in the United States: One diplomat assigned to the Libyan mission to the United Nations was expelled from the United States, and sixteen nonofficial Libyans were subpoenaed by a Grand Jury in connection with the plan.

In early January 1986 Libyan-U.S. tensions rose to new heights as Washington, having accused Libya of complicity in committing terrorist attacks in Europe, imposed new economic sanctions against Libya, and the U.S. Sixth Fleet put on a show of force in the Tripoli Flight Information Region. Qadhafi responded with relish to the international spotlight, despite his fears of military attack, and appealed to international opinion for support against the threats of a superpower.

In late March, however, U.S. warplanes bombed Libyan coastal missile sites and sank two Libyan patrol boats in the Gulf of Sidra. Then early on April 15, U.S. fighter bombers carried out attacks on targets in Libya, including military and residential sites in Tripoli and Banghazi. Perhaps 50 persons, most of them civilians, were killed in the attack. Among the casualties were Qadhafi's infant daughter, who was killed, and his two small sons—as well as a number of non-Libyans. The French, Finnish, and Austrian embassies in Tripoli were among the buildings demolished. According to President Reagan, the attack was in retaliation for Libyan sponsorship of the bombing of a Berlin disco some days earlier in which one U.S. serviceman was killed and over 200 other people were injured.

In a speech to the American people immediately following the April raid, Reagan promised further attacks on Libya if the Qadhafi regime did not cease its policy of terrorism against

Americans abroad. But it was clear that few persons, even within the Reagan administration, expected Qadhafi to change his behavior as a result of U.S. military action. The hope on the part of the Reagan administration was to hasten the demise of Qadhafi's regime. Instead, European and Arab observers were reinforced in their belief that the U.S. military action was a dangerous precedent and would lead to further violence in the region. Many Americans were likewise critical of official U.S. policy, pointing out that the administration had circumvented the requirement of the War Powers Act that Congress approve acts of war against other countries. Nonetheless, the majority of Americans appeared to support the attack.

Britain, which allowed the United States to fly aircraft from bases in the United Kingdom for the attack on Libya, was the only ally of the United States to approve the attack. The U.S. action brought severe criticism from other Europeans, many of whom agreed with British opposition leader Neil Kinnock that the U.S. military action was illegal under international law and, rather than preventing terrorism or constituting a suitable means of punishment for it, would further provoke terrorism. This view seemed to be supported by intelligence evidence of Libyan responsibility for the Berlin disco bombing, a reversion to direct attacks on U.S. targets generally avoided by Qadhafi since his 1981 plot to blow up the American Club in Khartoum. Under intense U.S. pressure, Qadhafi had apparently determined to retaliate via the only really effective weapon available to him: terrorism. Following the April raid he vowed publicly to continue to "export revolution." Reprisals against Americans and Britons began immediately: Three kidnapped Britons were executed in Beirut, an American working at the U.S. Embassy in Khartoum was shot and injured, threats were received against U.S. air bases in Britain, and a Libyan ship launched missiles against a U.S. Coast Guard station on Italy's island of Lampedusa.

EFFORTS TO EXPAND INFLUENCE
IN THE DEVELOPING WORLD

In recent years Qadhafi's anxiety over his international isolation has increased—as have his flamboyant rhetoric, his willingness to engage in disruptive and illegal acts, and his impatience with the failure to attain his goals. He has sought the favor of the developing world by endorsement of such Third World causes as the New International Economic Order, U.S. and Soviet bilateral disarmament, and ejection of Israel from the United Nations. But rejection by the Africans of Qadhafi's bid for the presidency of the Organization of African Unity in the early 1980s, as well as the negative reaction of other Third World states that were tentatively approached by Qadhafi in early 1985 concerning his desire for leadership of the Nonaligned Movement, underscored the caution with which even the Third World regards him.

Qadhafi's quest for international recognition has led him to engage in far-flung efforts to expand his influence in the Third World. In addition to his concentration of efforts on Africa and the Arab world, Qadhafi displayed a particular interest in Latin America during the early 1980s. And regarding Nicaragua and various small Caribbean countries, he has placed his major emphasis on attempts to fund opposition political figures and journalists. Moreover, limited numbers of Latin Americans, including Salvadorans, have been trained in Libya, and Qadhafi has supplied arms to Guatemalan and Salvadoran insurgents as well as to the Nicaraguan government. Libya also helped finance the controversial airport built by Cuban workers for the Marxist regime on Grenada (which was overthrown in the 1983 U.S. invasion) and secretly shipped arms, including Sam-7 missiles, to Argentina during the 1982 Falklands War. Concurrently, however, Tripoli has worked to strengthen diplomatic and trade relations with such major Latin American states as Brazil (from which Libya makes substantial military purchases), Mexico, and Argentina.

Libya's government-controlled Islamic Call Society, established in 1971 to encourage the spread of Islam—particularly in developing countries, where Muslims are in the minority—became much more active as an instrument of Libyan foreign policy in the mid-1980s, focusing its activities particularly on Africa and East Asia. Islamic Call has branches in Thailand, the Philippines, Malaysia, Indonesia, Australia, New Zealand, South Korea, Fiji, and New Caledonia, and it works with Libyan revolutionary committee members both to foster goodwill toward Libya and to provide assistance to antigovernment groups. In addition, Libya has long supported the Moro National Liberation Front, a Muslim separatist movement in the Philippines' Mindanao region. The Libyans are also thought to have provided training for Thai Muslim separatists belonging to the Pattani United Liberation Organization.

QADHAFI'S INCREASED ISOLATION

U.S. economic sanctions and military pressure against Libya have not only accentuated differences between the United States and its European allies over how best to deal with Qadhafi, but they have also helped Qadhafi project an image of victimization to the Third World. But Qadhafi has been unable to capture even Third World support for his anti-Western policies and maintains volatile relations even with other radical states such as Syria and Iran. Faced with growing international impatience with his actions and ideology, Qadhafi has placed himself in a corner from which he is unlikely to emerge into the international leadership position he covets.

Countries that do business or maintain correct diplomatic relations with Libya complain of the need to be constantly on guard against Qadhafi's pernicious demands and high-handed conduct. Those who seek to moderate his behavior—such as France, which tried to negotiate Libya out of Chad and was internationally embarrassed by Qadhafi's failure to live up to his agreement; and Morocco, which claimed that the 1984 unity agreement with Libya would moderate egregious Libyan activities—have reason to rue their public trust. Even Libya's valued ties to the Soviet Union are frequently tested severely both by Qadhafi's maverick policies and by his unwillingness to take Moscow's political sensitivities and economic needs into consideration.

Qadhafi's already-cited March 1985 speech underscored his feelings of vulnerability and his preoccupation with security, but it also indicated his intention, despite all, to apply more of the same policies that have worked to isolate both him and Libya. Chiding the Arabs for "throwing themselves at the

American White House," Qadhafi renewed his calls for Arab unity, yet promised to "go after and destroy" those who allow themselves to remain subservient to the United States. He also applauded a decision by the General People's Congress to place expanded police functions in the hands of the revolutionary committees and described vigilantism as the "legitimate and sacred right . . . [of] an entire people liquidating its opponents inside and abroad." Finally, ever the optimist, he claimed that despite threats from abroad, there is growing support from "revolutionary" states for an international united front against the United States.

NOTES

1. Useful discussions of Libyan foreign policy and foreign relations under Qadhafi can be found in John K. Cooley, *Libyan Sandstorm: The Complete Account of Qaddafi's Revolution;* Edward P. Haley, *Qaddafi and the U.S. Since 1969; Libya: A Country Study;* "The Libya Problem"; Lisa Anderson, "Qadhdhafi and the Kremlin"; and I. William Zartman and A. G. Kluge, "The Sources and Goals of Qaddafi's Foreign Policy." In addition, a survey of Qadhafi's foreign policy by Mary-Jane Deeb is forthcoming from Westview Press.

2. June 11, 1970, when the last Americans were withdrawn from Wheelus Air Base, which then became Okba bin Nafi Air Base, is celebrated as a Libyan national holiday.

3. Mohamed Heikal, *The Road to Ramadan,* p. 159.

4. Qadhafi, who has subsequently said publicly that he regrets having supported Idi Amin, claims he was misled by the Ugandan dictator's anti-Israelism into believing him to be a true progressive.

5. There is convincing evidence that Libya was responsible for the mid-1984 mining of the Red Sea and the Gulf of Suez. The Libyan roll-on/roll-off ship—the *Ghat*—transitted the Suez Canal southbound on July 6 and unloaded its cargo in Assab, Ethiopia, some time between July 9 and 17. On its trip through the area in which other ships later hit mines, the *Ghat* was observed moving at a speed considerably slower than its normal transit speed. Before the *Ghat* turned to transit north through the Suez Canal on July 29, it was sighted by the French near Aden. Only a few days after the return transit of the *Ghat*, the first of eleven ships to hit mines did so in the area through which the Libyan ship had traveled. Taken to France for repairs upon return, the *Ghat* was discovered to have

a damaged cargo door, the result of it having been opened at sea. Before, and then after, the July voyage to the Red Sea, the entire *Ghat* crew had been changed: The original crew was of mixed nationality, whereas the crew that had taken the July trip through the Red Sea and Gulf of Suez was composed entirely of Libyans. The mine retrieved by the British mine-sweeping team was found to be a Soviet mine of the type purchased from Eastern Europe by the Libyans.

6. Although it appears likely that the U.S. government may have warned Qadhafi about a planned antigovernment plot in 1971, the claim in some Arab circles that Qadhafi's 1969 coup was sponsored by the United States is beyond belief. According to this theory, the United States' purpose in bringing Qadhafi to power was to gain access to Libyan oil and to keep Qadhafi embroiled with his neighbors and hence not a threat to Israel. There is no evidence to support this claim.

6

Libya's Economy: The Troubled Superstructure

Except for oil wealth, the story of the Libyan economy is not a story of success. Libya is a land with few natural resources other than petroleum, in which limited agricultural areas have remained relatively underdeveloped, and where severely limited water resources have been chronically abused. Despite a dramatic improvement in the average living standard since the 1969 revolution, owing to the regime's distributive policies, none of the country's fundamental economic problems have changed for the better. Libya remains a country with little industrial infrastructure and very limited supplies of technological and managerial skills. The mid- to long-term economic prognosis is very uncertain given the downward trend in international oil prices and the lack of a substitute for oil as a source of national income.

Unlike certain other petroleum-rich states, Libya does have potential for development of agriculture and small industries. The fertile, though narrow, coastal strip has in the past adequately sustained a flourishing population. The country's sunny climate and central position on the Mediterranean coastline provide excellent opportunities for the development of tourism, shipping, and trading industries of the sort that flourished in Lebanon before 1975. And the enormous injection of petroleum wealth beginning in the early 1960s provided Libya with vast capital resources for development.

But Libya has had neither the technical nor the human resources to transform capital into a productive base. As in other Middle Eastern oil-producing countries, the most beneficial results of oil wealth have been a tremendous expansion of social services, including education. But neither the monarchy nor Qadhafi's subsequent regime has been able adequately to exploit Libya's economic potential. Libya not only remains critically dependent on one valuable but expendable natural resource, but it must also rely on large numbers of foreigners to operate its economy and on foreign imports for some 65 percent of its food. The economic results of Libya's oil revolution remain doubtful at best.

THE PETROLEUM-BASED ECONOMY

Petroleum was first discovered in Libya in exploitable quantities in 1959, and by the mid-1960s the influence of petroleum wealth had begun to be felt. The 1950 gross domestic product (GDP) of about $40 per capita climbed to nearly $5,000 in 1975 and had reached almost $11,000 for each Libyan by 1980. Despite massive spending on ambitious development projects, foreign exchange reserves mounted, reaching a high point of over $14 billion in 1981. Of a total GDP of over $34 billion in 1980, some 65 percent was in oil income, with the remainder from the commercial and financial sector, including housing, public services, and transportation. (As a result of the decline in world oil prices, petroleum accounted for only 47 percent of the $25 billion GDP in 1985). In a short amount of time, Libya was transformed from a literally dirt-poor desert country whose main source of income after World War II was the sale of military scrap iron, into what is technically known as a "rentier state"—a country with a low level of social and economic development that is suddenly catapulted into wealth because of a valuable and plentiful natural resource. Under these circumstances there was a sudden great rise in per capita income, but the social and organizational changes necessary for sustainable economic growth did not occur.

Although Libya's petroleum resources are not so vast as those of states such as Kuwait and Saudi Arabia, it does possess extensive oil reserves (approximately 22 billion barrels), which at present production levels should provide considerable income for at least the next forty years. Recognizing the expendability of the petroleum resource, all modern Libyan economic plans, including the five-year plan of 1981–1985, have sought to steer Libya away from dependence on petroleum. Yet as of the end of this most recent five-year economic plan, income from exported crude petroleum constituted approximately 80 percent of government revenues as well as virtually all foreign exchange earnings. Moreover, continued high rates of spending, technical difficulties, poor financial management, and lower international oil demand with consequently lower prices have severely depleted the country's monetary reserves.

The most evident cause of Libya's current economic difficulties was the decline in world petroleum prices after 1981. Since the spring of 1983 Libyan petroleum production has remained near Libya's OPEC quota of 999,000 barrels per day (bpd), a sharp decline from the 1.83 million bpd produced in 1980. Moreover, the early 1986 average price for Libyan crude of $27 or $28 per barrel was in sharp contrast to the 1980 price of $40 per barrel. By the beginning of 1985, liquid foreign exchange reserves had plunged to $3 billion—from $13 billion in 1980. This was about enough to provide four months of import coverage at present reduced levels. Moreover, it has been rumored that, for the first time since the 1969 revolution, Libya might have to engage in foreign borrowing—a position of dependence that Qadhafi has sought to avoid. In order to arrest the foreign exchange drawdown (and to satisfy overdue bills for imported goods and services), Libya began to produce about 150,000 bpd above its OPEC quota. By late 1985, despite a current-account deficit of some $1.2 billion, the country's foreign exchange reserves had been raised to about $3.5 billion. But Libyan vulnerability to the vicissitudes of the international petroleum market was painfully evident.

Nonetheless, fluctuation in the international petroleum market is only the precipitating factor for present economic difficulties. The failure to develop a viable industrial or agricultural base as well as the massive misuse of funds not only for arms purchases but also for poorly conceived efforts to develop nonpetroleum sectors of the economy are likewise at fault. Moreover, operating costs and consumption expenditures have continued to take priority over domestic investments, and Qadhafi's economic dictates have served to undercut the developing commercial class, thereby stifling incentive and virtually eliminating free enterprise. The country's revolutionary economic procedures and philosophies have sharply limited international investment in Libya and have even undercut tourism.

ECONOMIC GOALS OF THE REVOLUTION

Qadhafi is aware that Libya's economy undergirds his domestic as well as his foreign policy goals. Much of his philosophy as expounded in the "Green Book" pertains to steering an alternative course between capitalist and Marxist economics. He regards a strong economy as the key to Libya's future security and significance and has sought to use the national economy to secure for Libya a position as an independent and powerful international actor. Laws decree that 15 percent of the yearly oil revenues be reserved and that at least 70 percent of the remainder be devoted to development projects. But although extensive efforts have been made by the revolutionary regime to use national resources to benefit the Libyan people, insufficient indigenous technical personnel, incorrect planning, ill-advised spending, and, most of all, the lack of a comprehensive and realistic development strategy have all contributed to Libya's present state of economic deterioration and, in some sectors, near chaos.

Following an initial period of economic assessment after the revolution, described by John Wright as "two years of economic stagnation,"[1] the new regime began a series of measures intended to move the country toward Qadhafi's eventual goal of "socialism." This process has been gradual and reflects the evolution of Qadhafi's ideology and the serial publication of his three-part "Green Book."[2] Qadhafi's overall goals for Libya have been dealt with in previous chapters. As noted, he essentially seeks to erase the effects of past exploitation, placing Libyans in charge of their own future. In order to do so, he aims for a more equitable distribution of income and services, greater government control of the economy, and independence from foreign influence. And to achieve these ends, he has sought to make Libya self-sufficient both in agriculture and industry and to educate Libyans to provide their own technical expertise. The two major economic obstacles to these goals that Qadhafi identified upon coming to power were foreign capitalists and traditional domestic elites. Implementation of policies leading in the 1970s to the nationalization of all services and production were intended both to shake off foreign influence and to redistribute wealth to the disadvantage of the traditional Libyan elite. For the revolutionary regime, the latter represented not only a class of "collaborators" with past colonialist masters but also a group whose wealth provided its members with an independent influence base of potential threat to the revolution.

The international petroleum companies were Qadhafi's first targets. Although Libya had managed to better its profit-sharing arrangements with the petroleum-producing companies after joining OPEC in 1962, the revolutionary regime desired ultimate control of its petroleum industry and a greater share of petroleum income. Qadhafi moved cautiously on the issue of nationalization, however, to avoid damage to Libya and to get the best deals possible from the divided petroleum companies. Geographically close to Europe and producing high-grade "sweet" crude (petroleum with a low wax content), Libya by 1970 was already in the favorable position of supplying roughly one-third of western European petroleum imports. It remains a Libyan paradox that Qadhafi, despite his anti-Western and anticapitalist rhetoric, has even today not opted for complete nationalization—in contrast to the leaders of more "capitalist" nations such as Saudi Arabia, Kuwait, and prerevolutionary Iran.

The revolutionary Libyan regime concentrated first on the weaker independent petroleum companies, then moved on to the majors.[3] Government-ordered production cutbacks in 1970 increased pressure on the producers, leading to negotiations in February 1971 that produced the Tripoli Agreements whereby Libyan revenues were increased by one-half. By 1973, through partial and in some cases complete nationalization procedures, Libya had achieved a controlling interest in all petroleum companies operating in Libya. In September, 51 percent of all foreign oil company holdings in Libya were nationalized. By 1974 the Libyan government held approximately 60 percent of the country's petroleum production but, acknowledging Libya's lack of technical expertise, had entered into sharing agreements with several major producers. Meanwhile, foreign banks were nationalized and all foreign investments in Libya put under strict controls. As was to be expected, Libya under Qadhafi was among the first of the petroleum states to recognize the potential of the "oil weapon," making use of it from 1971 on. During the 1973 Middle East War, Libya supported the oil cutbacks directed against the West and did not resume sales to the United States until March 1974.

Under the 1971–1975 Five-Year Economic Plan, the Libyan government initiated efforts to limit oil production in order to preserve resources for the future. However, these efforts soon ran into difficulty because of popular unwillingness to accept reductions in generous government-spending programs. A 1975 oil production cut to one-third the 1969 level was shortly rescinded because of popular discontent over a resultant cut in social welfare benefits.

Despite the tightened restrictions on individual economic activities, it was not until the late 1970s that Qadhafi turned his full attention to the problem of unequal distribution of wealth. Measures taken almost immediately after the revolution to raise the general living standard included not only the beginning of a variety of social, educational, and health-care services but also a 50 percent across-the-board increase in the wages of all Libyan workers. Rapid construction projects were implemented to provide adequate housing for all Libyans. But there remained the problem of accumulation of wealth by an elite group of Libyans who, although they paid lip service to the revolution and had in most cases trimmed their formerly opulent life-styles, were not only still wealthy by ordinary standards but considered tainted by past acts and associations as well. Having dealt with the external exploiters, Qadhafi turned to the internal.

Three areas drew the regime's attention: buildings, land, and capital—the three repositories of most indigenous wealth. Basically antagonistic to money—as well as to merchants, profits, and investment—Qadhafi sought to transform Libya into a society in which individual profit and eventually even money would be eliminated. In 1977, concurrent with publication of the "Green Book," Part 2, it was decreed that no Libyan family, with the exception of those having sons over 18, would be allowed to own more than one dwelling place. Ownership of rental properties was given to the occupants, resulting in tremendous loss of investment for the wealthy and middle classes—as well as for some members of the poorer class. With all classes of Libyans thus affected, the pace of popular disillusionment with the revolution was significantly accelerated.

Then, within a year, the government increased rates of land confiscation and reallocation, seeking to redistribute all holdings of more than 24.7 acres (10 hectares), considered to be the amount of land that one family could farm without hiring outside labor. This program, though implemented in some areas, has met such widespread resistance by landowners that by the mid-1980s it had not been fully carried out. Nonetheless, wealthy individuals as well as wealthy tribes have been severely disadvantaged both economically and politically by the program.

Further measures followed. In the late 1970s, Qadhafi's belief that self-management requires elimination of employees led to popular takeovers of many businesses, including some government-operated services such as utilities. (The production and management difficulties that have resulted from popular operation of less critical economic sectors provide a clue as to why the country's key petroleum, banking, and insurance enterprises have remained generally exempt from popular takeover.) In 1978 retail trade was declared abolished, and the merchant class was described as parasitical and exploitative of society. Most private business establishments have since closed, and Tripoli is today probably the only Arab capital without colorful *souks* (bazaars). Then, in March 1980, an official decree eliminated private sources of savings, a development that effectively removed the wealth of all Libyans except those with funds abroad. All old bills above 1 dinar were collected by the banks, and no Libyan was allowed to withdraw—or hold—more than 1,000 of the new dinars.

TABLE 6.1
Libya's principal trading partners in 1984
(in millions of dollars)

	Libyan Exports	Libyan Imports
Italy	2,527	1,826
West Germany	1,996	885
Spain	969	293
France	753	233
Turkey	655	155
Yugoslavia	407	225
Switzerland	402	110
Netherlands	366	204
Greece	326	120
Romania	311	140

Source: International Monetary Fund Direction of Trade
Statistics Yearbook, 1985. (No figures on Libyan trade with
the Soviet Union are available. Such trade, which amounts to
several billions of dollars yearly, is mainly in the form of
Libyan arms purchases.)

SEEKING TO BENEFIT FROM OIL WEALTH

Beginning in the mid-1970s Libya began to use some of its petroleum income to make major investments in the industrialized countries, particularly in Europe (see Table 6.1). In 1976 the Libyan Arab Foreign Bank purchased a 9.5 percent interest in Fiat of Italy as well as a large share in the Ente Nazionale Idrocarburi (ENI). By early 1986 Libya was believed to own 15 percent of the giant Fiat corporation. In addition, significant Libyan government purchases of real estate have been transacted in both Italy and Malta. Nonetheless, most of the new wealth has been spent at home. The early years of the Qadhafi regime were, in fact, a time of almost frenzied spending as government ministries sought new projects in the hope that major investments would lead to progress and development. The Five-Year Economic and Social Transformation Plan adopted in 1976 gave priority to development of agriculture, industry, electricity, education, municipalities, and housing.

Since the revolution, the agricultural sector has received more economic development funds than any other sector of the economy. But ill-advised agricultural projects have brought a series of environmental disasters, including extensive degradation of pasture land, the full impact of which is yet to be realized. Libya's efforts to become self-sufficient in food production led to a series of extremely expensive experiments—including efforts to raise sheep at the Kufra Oasis and to grow wheat on the Gefara Plain—that were subsequently revealed to be economically and environmentally unsound. Massive transportation and feeding costs made the Kufra-grown mutton more expensive than imports from abroad and led to cancellation of the project. And Gefara, a region of little rainfall, was eventually recognized as best suited to its previous use: camel grazing.

Agricultural development efforts have also resulted in a further lowering of the water table, especially in coastal areas; as a result, Tripoli in particular now suffers from an infusion of salt water into underground reserves. In the late 1970s water-intensive crops had to be discontinued in some areas because of the falling water table. In other areas, salination forced discontinuation of pilot projects. Confiscation of tribal lands "not in use" for redistribution to small farmers did not lead to any significant increase in agricultural production as the rural poor preferred in many cases to leave the land for a better life in the cities. In short, by the mid-1980s the contribution of agriculture to the GNP showed little sign of improvement.

Government efforts to develop industry have likewise been generally unsuccessful, despite massive funding for a variety of projects including textiles, electrical machinery, milling, and food processing. Some small industries involving food processing, textiles, and handicrafts have appeared since the revolution. But in many cases inferior products offered at prices higher than those for similar imports have been rejected by purchasers. Moreover, corruption, denounced as an evil carryover from former times, has not been eliminated. Many heavily subsidized ventures have not moved beyond the planning stage despite considerable optimistic rhetoric and large infusions of funds.

The petroleum and construction industries have expanded considerably, despite continued reliance on more foreign than Libyan employees; elsewhere, however, lack of resources or of markets for manufactured goods, as well as insufficient numbers of qualified technical personnel and poor management, have resulted in notable failures. In early 1985 the main contractor for the $1 billion Ras Lanouf petrochemical project southwest of Banghazi was reportedly threatening to take the Libyan government to the International Chamber of Commerce arbitration court in Paris for nonpayment of over $20 million in fees. Although the Ras Lanouf refinery was eventually completed in late 1985, it was several years behind schedule and, despite optimistic official pronouncements, other massive projects, including a steel mill at Misratah and an aluminum smelter at Zawiyah, languished in an incomplete state.

STATE OF THE LIBYAN ECONOMY

In his revolution day speech of September 1, 1985, Qadhafi called on the Libyan people to be willing to suffer in support of the state. Although this exhortation represented a tacit admission of the country's deepening economic difficulties, Qadhafi continued to deny elsewhere that Libya is threatened by an economic crisis or that cuts in oil revenues have affected the lives of all Libyans. Nonetheless, by the end of 1985 Libyan imports had been cut to $7 billion and exports to $10 billion from 1980 peaks of almost $16 billion and $22 billion, respectively. Furthermore, the GDP was down to about $7,000 per capita, and the total GDP had fallen to $25 billion. According to *Africa Confidential*, the 1985 budget adopted by the General People's Congress reduced administrative expenditures by 17 percent to $4 billion and development expenditures by 19 percent to $5.7 billion.[4] In fact, the cuts may be considerably larger.

Despite troubled commercial relations, Libya continues to trade with a variety of nations, particularly the Europeans. Between $1.5–2 billion was spent on arms purchases in 1985, mainly from the Soviet Union.[5] In Western Europe, Italy is Libya's closest trading partner, with West Germany a distant second; the former exported over $1.3 billion to Libya in 1985 and imported almost $2.5 billion. Spain, France, Turkey, Switzerland, the Netherlands, Greece, and the U.K. also have significant trade relations with Libya, mainly importing petroleum and exporting technology, technicians, and consumables. Some

15,000 Italians work in Libya, as do about 5,000 Britons and several thousand representatives of other western European nationalities.

U.S. economic sanctions against Libya were first instituted in the mid-1970s, and since 1978 the export to Libya of many categories of U.S. equipment, including all aircraft and military and nuclear equipment, has routinely been denied. A 1982 embargo on imports of Libyan crude oil brought to a halt Libyan exports of some 40 percent of its petroleum production to the United States (representing about 15 percent of U.S. imports). Despite U.S. trade sanctions against Libya, the U.S. Department of Commerce reported an increase in U.S. sales to Libya in 1985—totaling nearly $260 million, mainly in machinery and agricultural products. An absolute, but relatively inconsequential, jump in U.S. imports from Libya ($9.5 million in 1984 to more than $37 million in 1985, mostly in refined petroleum products) was halted by the imposition in November 1985 of U.S. restrictions on imports of refined Libyan petroleum products—at the same time as Libya's Ras Lanouf refinery was coming into operation. Nonetheless, a variety of U.S. companies—including four major petroleum companies—continued to do business in Libya.

A near total embargo on commercial relations with Libya, long prevented by U.S. business interests, was legislated by the Reagan administration in January 1986 under authority of the International Emergency Economic Powers Act. The measure applied a virtually complete ban on economic transactions with Libya by American citizens and froze some $200 million in Libyan assets in the United States. The results of the imposition of new U.S. sanctions on trade with Libya have yet to become clear, including the question of whether Libya will move to freeze U.S. assets, which total around $1 billion. In early 1986 some 800 to 1,000 Americans lived in Libya, the majority employed despite U.S. prohibitions. Qadhafi's treatment of these persons has been exemplary—an apparent effort to put the lie to U.S. warnings that American citizens in Libya are potential hostages to Qadhafi's policies.

Although the Libyan oil-exploration budget was increased in the mid-1980s and completion of the Ras Lanouf refinery constituted a major triumph, the critical Libyan petroleum industry faced an uncertain future. Libyan crude remained in high demand, but in early 1986 the industry suffered a variety of problems including low standards of maintenance of facilities and pipelines, unsatisfactory safety standards, and insufficient qualified personnel due to lower salaries. Considerable amounts of petroleum continued to be lost through mismanagement, and a variety of disputes between the Libyan National Oil Company and foreign producers hampered some operations.

Internal Impact

Clearly the Libyan economy is in trouble, but the government appears uncertain as to how to get out of its dilemma. The first line of defense has been broad austerity measures. Since 1980 financial difficulties have led to severe reduction of imported goods, cuts in administrative budgets and government salaries, recall of students from study abroad, expulsions of foreign workers, and increased restrictions on travel and on the amount of money that can be taken out of the country. Since 1984 virtual suspension of spare parts purchases has caused hardship in nearly all elements of the economy. Housing, agriculture, and heavy industry are receiving lower levels of funding, and no significant new agricultural project has been completed since 1981.

Moreover, financial difficulties appear to have exacerbated corruption and graft. Government exhortations reflect mounting official concern over patronage and black marketeering as well as over falsification of production figures in order to allege quota fulfillment. The prevalence of black markets, many of which trafficked in U.S. dollars, was by 1984 resulting in the loss of money by state markets and cooperatives. By late 1985 few items other than food were available for Libyan dinars, and there were periodic purges of agricultural and other government offices in an effort to stem corruption and to reduce dependence on food imports.

Selected projects continued to receive preferential funding, although even here payment was frequently tardy. Post-1980 economic difficulties have brought a significant decline in arms purchases, although Qadhafi continued to give priority to military spending. An early 1985 slowdown in arms deliveries from the Soviet Union appeared to reflect disagreements with Moscow over nonpayment of some $7 billion for arms already delivered in addition to Libyan efforts to pay for ever-increasing amounts of goods and services in petroleum. Nonetheless, Qadhafi's visit to Moscow in late 1985 brought apparent agreement for resumption of arms transfers, including the expensive SA-5 missile system—a subsequent source of intensified controversy between Libya and its neighbors as well as between Libya and the United States.

But Qadhafi's pet project, above all, is the "Great Manmade River (GMMR)." Completion of this ambitious groundwater-supply project by the South Korean construction firm Dong Ah will, according to some estimates, cost Libya more than $25 billion. Initiated in August 1984, the Great Manmade River was not scheduled for completion until 1997, at which time it is anticipated that some 7,800,000 cubic yards (about 6 million cubic meters) of water per day will be delivered via several thousand miles of underground pipeline from Libya's extensive underground water resources to the country's coastal cities and agricultural developments. It is also hoped that by 1989 some parts of the massive system will come into service to relieve near-critical problems of water shortage and water contamination, particularly in Tripoli.

The size of the undertaking and the expense involved make it increasingly doubtful that the project will be completed, although in early 1986 stage one was well under way. Estimates of the ultimate cost have continued to rise, and, in addition to being economically unsound, the scheme may turn out to be environmentally disastrous as a result of further lowering of the water table. Qadhafi appears, nonetheless, to be staking his hopes for Libyan economic independence on successful completion of the project, despite evidence that the GMMR could have serious effects on other aspects of the economy and thus further deplete Libya's financial reserves.

Impact on Foreign Relations

Libya's economic pinch has not brought a noticeable decline in Qadhafi's support for revolutionary and oppositionist groups around the world, most of which involves low amounts of funding. But economic difficulties have begun seriously to affect Libya's foreign as well as domestic policies. The impact of Libya's economic difficulties has been felt outside Libya in the form of reductions in the size of Libyan diplomatic missions and draw-downs in contributions to international organizations, including UN affiliates. Strains have been created in relations with other countries over nonpayment of debts and attempts by the Libyans to use their arrearages to extract political and commercial concessions. According to press reports, a senior official of the Association of Turkish Contractors complained in early 1985 that the Libyan government had decided to halt 400 construction projects, over 180 of them with Turkish firms and many only half-finished because of financial difficulties.

Expulsion of foreign workers in 1985 also severely strained ties with several countries, particularly Tunisia and Egypt. The Libyan government sought to portray the move as a natural termination of contracts and publicly described the "failure to renew contracts" as an attempt to impel the Libyan people to control their own economy. It was evident, however, that economic stringency measures were a major factor in the decision to expel the guest workers. Although unskilled labor was the major target of the expulsion order, foreign experts such as teachers and medical personnel have become increasingly apprehensive about their future in Libya, particularly as the regime has issued tighter controls on export of funds. Many have left the country. But Libyan dependence on foreign skills and the unemployment problems in many Arab and eastern European countries ensure continued involvement of large numbers of foreign workers in the Libyan economy.

In addition to the expulsion of at least 60,000 foreign workers in 1985, efforts were made to reduce foreign economic presence. Foreign companies faced increased pressures to "Libyanize" through the training of Libyan workers to take over technical and administrative functions. The serious payment arrearages to foreign companies that had occurred over the past several years worsened as Libya increased its efforts to pay for services with petroleum. This policy has worked a particular hardship on eastern European countries, for all of which Libya is a major employer and a source of hard-currency earnings. Some 30,000 Bulgarians, Poles, and Romanians are involved in Libyan military and economic projects such as road building, agricultural development, and building construction. Increased restrictions on salary transfers out of Libya and demands that petroleum be accepted as payment for goods as well as labor have caused acrimonious exchanges between the Libyan and other governments.

The Prognosis

The gap between raised domestic expectations and the Libyan government's current inability to provide could have a significant impact on the viability of the regime. For the present, however, the Libyan people have accepted, more with passive anger than with action, tax and price increases, wage freezes, reductions in government pensions, severe cutbacks in imports, and shortfalls of consumer goods. In addition to their fear of reprisal from police and security forces, they retain a collective memory of the significant increase that has occurred in the average standard of living since the revolution as well as a hope that the decline in oil revenues will be a temporary phenomenon. Other than private grumbling and questioning of the motives and policies of the regime, most Libyans remain largely quiescent.

Nevertheless, frustration and discontent have reached high levels, which apparently are continuing to rise as shortages of water, food, and electricity become commonplace. Isolated attacks on government stores and sporadic outbursts of violence—sometimes leading to deaths—have occasionally occurred among consumers, who must constantly queue up during basic daily shopping trips.

More serious still, economic disagreement has continued to feed political infighting in the Libyan hierarchy. Disagreements over economic policy lay at the base of the 1975 coup attempt by Qadhafi's ministers of planning and foreign affairs. Their failure and flight from the country resulted in virtual elimination of moderate voices in the Libyan leadership, providing Qadhafi greater liberty to proceed with his economic plans. By the mid-1980s, as the pinch of reduced revenues was becoming sharply felt, a struggle for control of funds emerged that not only pitted revolutionary committee members against the more formal government structure but also appeared to have penetrated even into Qadhafi's inner circle. Sirte Military District Commander Hassan Askhal, a member of Qadhafi's tribe, was apparently murdered in late 1985 in a dispute that, although the details are fuzzy, probably included disagreement within the leadership over use of government revenues.

Political disagreement over the use of funds is rather more significant than the low morale, grumbling, and commodity hoarding that characterized the majority reaction to economic difficulties. It can plausibly be argued that Qadhafi does not need a great deal of money to remain in power. Indeed, Qadhafi would actually prefer to *eliminate* money, despite his recognition of the importance of a stable economy. Nonetheless, if the country's economic difficulties make it impossible for Qadhafi to ensure continuation of the system of privileges and perks that keeps much of the military quiescent, or if declining revenues continue to generate infighting within the inner circle, the regime's tenure is definitely endangered. Whatever Libya's political future, the perennial economic question will remain: how to move away from a petroleum-based economy into balanced growth and development.

NOTES

1. John Wright, *Libya: A Modern History*, p. 262.

2. The concept of socialism was not, in fact, incorporated into the name of the country until 1977, when the Libyan Arab Republic became the Socialist People's Libyan Arab Jamahiriyyah.

3. For a full description of the Libyan petroleum industry, see Frank C. Waddams, *The Libyan Oil Industry*, and J. A. Allan, *Libya: The Experience of Oil*.

4. *Africa Confidential* (London, March 13, 1985), pp. 3, 4, reprinted in *Joint Publications Research Service—Near East* (April 15, 1985).

5. Since 1970 Libya has spent a total of some $29 billion on arms, including all military goods and services. Less than 30 percent of that amount represents purchases from the West.

7
Prospects for the Future

Several conclusions about present-day Libya are immediately apparent. Foremost among them is the centrality of Qadhafi to the country's political, social, and economic systems. Without Qadhafi, Libya would clearly be a different country. Yet despite Qadhafi's reorganization of Libyan society and the significant postrevolution improvements in social welfare benefits and standard of living, it is evident that the Libyan revolution has failed to achieve its major goals. The Libyan people continue to respond half-heartedly to Qadhafi's revolutionary philosophy, the world has not accepted him as a great political and economic thinker, the Arabs have rejected his efforts to "unify by force," a Palestinian state has not replaced Israel, and the West has not been punished for its colonialist arrogance.

The continuing importance of oil wealth to Qadhafi's political experiment is another central factor in modern Libyan life. Troubled though the Libyan economy may be, the country's petroleum income remains the pillar on which Qadhafi's tenure rests. Oil wealth continues to provide him the means to maintain his security forces, to indulge in extravagant military purchases, to keep the Libyan military largely quiescent through an extensive system of perquisites, and to provide sufficient welfare benefits to convince at least a sizable majority of the Libyans that the egalitarian "state of the masses" is a positive successor to the previous Libyan government.

But Qadhafi looks back with obvious impatience and apparently increasing frustration on his failure to achieve the ideals he set out in the "Green Book." The consequence has been a growing radicalism within the Libyan system, as Qadhafi has

125

begun in recent years to rely on the youthful members of the revolutionary committee system to promote his programs. Meanwhile, internal political extremism and, for at least some Libyans, foreign adventurism have combined with the economic austerity programs implemented during the early 1980s to stimulate mounting internal unhappiness with Qadhafi's continued tenure.

As the greater part of success has evaded him, Qadhafi's anger against the Libyan dissidents and others who oppose him has deepened, resulting in a more aggressive and violent foreign policy that includes not only attacks on Libyan oppositionists abroad but also growing involvement with international terrorism as a substitute for state power.

Qadhafi is pleased that his policies have extended the impact of the Libyan revolution to most parts of the world. His ability to preoccupy the United States, and to drive a wedge among the Western allies and between the United States and the moderate Arabs over the issue of economic sanctions against Libya, has gratified him. Lack of international consensus on how significant a threat Qadhafi's policies actually pose to the international community has served to shield Libya from retaliation for economic high-handedness and the export of violence. More important, however, Libya's continuing ability to export high-quality petroleum, to grant lucrative technological and construction contracts, and to absorb large numbers of workers from Europe and the Arab world has saved Libya from international isolation.

Yet, instead of bringing Qadhafi closer to fulfillment of his goals, the Libyan flouting of international norms has increased Libya's political and social isolation and harmed its prospects for economic development. Instead of rising to a position of international leadership, as Qadhafi had hoped, Libya is regarded with mounting wariness, even by other Arabs. Such near-universal suspicion and disapproval raises the odds that international opinion could eventually unite to apply pressures on Libya through either multilateral economic boycott, ejection from international organizations, or even military means.

Qadhafi's methods have harmed the very causes he espouses. Other Arabs agree with Qadhafi that failure to resolve the Palestine question lies at the root of international terrorism, especially terrorism against Western and Israeli targets. But Qadhafi's efforts have reinforced Western prejudices against Arabs by holding before the world the image of the Arab as terrorist and fanatic, a concept ultimately far more damaging to both Libya and the Arabs in general than the continued existence of the state of Israel—for whom international perception of the Arabs as radicals is actually a political bonus.

Yet despite the fact that Qadhafi's tenure is apparently not immediately threatened from within or without, the Libyan revolution may have reached a critical stage. Qadhafi faces continuing, and in some areas increased, difficulty in forcing the nonpoliticized Libyan people to comply with his economic and social theories. External and internal unhappiness against his rule is growing, and present problems can be expected to multiply at a faster pace in coming years. Indeed, a growing number of observers do not expect his tenure to last through 1987.

ECONOMIC PROSPECTS

The Libyan people are disgruntled over the decline in their standard of living in the early 1980s. Yet, although economic problems and radical domestic policies will likely exacerbate the people's frustration with Qadhafi, they are unlikely in themselves to destabilize the regime. Petroleum income of some $8–10 billion per year will continue to enable Qadhafi to meet most of his expenses. Hence Libya is not likely to go bankrupt, despite fluctuations in the international petroleum market and large-scale spending and mismanagement at the national level. Nor will unilateral economic boycotts by other countries have a significant further impact on the Libyan economy. The United States' refusal to sell parts and technology or to allow American citizens to work in Libya has done some limited and short-term damage to the Libyan economy. But, by and large, Europeans and others have picked up the extra business and provided the needed expertise and equipment.

Nonetheless, the central problem posed by the lack of alternate resources to petroleum remains unresolved, and the long debate continues over how best to make petroleum wealth serve Libya's national interest. The drop in financial resources has apparently stimulated competition in the inner circle over access to more limited funds—with possible serious political implications, as discussed earlier. Qadhafi's dedication to massive spending on military armaments appears to be above public debate and will continue to absorb funds needed elsewhere. Despite economic austerity programs, large-scale agricultural and industrial self-sufficiency projects will likewise receive priority. But the prospect that Libya will soon overcome its massive dependence on imported food or develop a competitive industrial base is not good.

The regime is failing, furthermore, to deal with an accelerated alienation of the Libyan people—particularly technocrats, intellectuals, management, and business personnel who disapprove of the means of economic management of the country and resent the international pariah image that Qadhafi's policies have earned. The continued flight of educated Libyans from their country at a time when Qadhafi seeks to eliminate reliance on foreign expertise bodes ill for Libya's economic future. A dramatic drop in the number of Libyan students abroad, for financial as well as political reasons, indicates that the problem of insufficient trained Libyans will not be resolved soon. For the foreseeable future, Libya can be expected to remain dependent on foreign expertise for its educational and medical systems as well as for its petroleum industry and fledgling industrial infrastructure. But the regime's attempts at "Libyanization" of business and industry will probably continue to lower managerial competence and production quotas.

SOCIAL PROSPECTS

Libyan society remains deeply conservative and resistant to change. Many Libyans continue to resent the regime's efforts to replace traditional leadership elites, to enlist women into professional and military life, to participate in politics, or even to create a national as opposed to a family, tribal, or regional identity. More serious still, the petroleum-based social welfare state has stimulated economic dependence and lack of ambition on the part of many Libyans, as attested by frequent official exhortations to citizens to assume social and economic leadership and responsibility.

Except in the work of a few researchers such as Marius and Mary-Jane Deeb, the social effects of Qadhafi's revolution on the Libyan people have not been carefully examined. Few studies have been allowed. Certainly, however, some of these effects must be profound, particularly for women and the newly urbanized people whose lives have been significantly changed during recent years. The impact of compulsory education and the rise in literacy will also influence Libya's future—as will the fact that 50 percent of Libyans are under 15 and cannot remember a time when Qadhafi was not in charge. These young people are often strongly tempted to participate in political extremism, which, if nothing else, lends a bit of excitement to lives that are otherwise rather lack-luster owing to economic and social constraints. Yet despite the growing feelings of nationalism among Libyans—particularly when the country is threatened from outside—it is likely that most Libyans remain unconvinced by Qadhafi's philosophies. The average Libyans continue, as do ordinary people everywhere, to prefer luxury to austerity, and their political responses are more likely to be passive than active.

In his article in the *Middle East Journal* analyzing the political development of Libya in historical perspective, Jacques Roumani points out that whatever the outcome of the Libyan revolution, and whatever Libya's political future, Qadhafi's revolution has given to the Libyan people the opportunity to come to terms with their past, particularly the oppressive colonial past that unleashed strong pan-Arab and pan-Islamic response.[1] Unfortunately, life in the *Jamahiriyya* has probably done much to reinforce in young Libyans the propensity to blame outsiders for the country's continued inability to achieve its potential. Qadhafi's constant emphasis on the historical wronging of Libya has tended to shift the focus of the people from present responsibility to demands for retribution for the colonialist and imperialist past.

POLITICAL PROSPECTS

How long Qadhafi will remain central to Libya's future remains uncertain. His prospects for continuation as Libya's leader over at least the short term are fairly good, despite rising tensions in his inner circle and growing unhappiness and periodic coup plotting in the military. Popular malaise over Qadhafi's policies is countered by the effective and multilayered Libyan security services and by the Libyan people's general lack of motivation toward political activism. There is no possibility that Qadhafi will be voted out of office, and almost none that a popular rising will unseat him. Nor does there appear to be significant cooperation between his external and internal opponents: Both groups remain weak and disunited.

Qadhafi has for several years proven his ability to cover his tracks and is a past master of stopping just short of provoking his adversaries to action. His confidence in his ability to continue to operate with impunity was heightened in 1984 by Libya's successful mining of the Red Sea and the Gulf of Suez, followed by his escape from retaliation over Libya's broken promise to withdraw its forces from Chad. But Qadhafi's impatience over the failure to achieve his ultimate goals could lead him to take imprudent action on the international level—action that could bring massive retaliation from outside Libya. He was clearly shaken by the U.S. military action against Libya in early 1986, but he remains unrepentant and determined to stay the course he has set.

Nor could any nation mounting a military attack on Qadhafi expect cooperation from Qadhafi's fellow Libyans. Fears of a U.S. military action against Libya in January 1986, followed by U.S. air strikes in March and April, rallied throngs of Libyan revolutionaries to their leader and elicited warnings to the United States from several Arab states as well as from Libyan oppositionist groups in exile. A recent issue of the Libyan National Salvation Front newsletter declared that the only way for non-Libyans to deal with Qadhafi is by boycotting the regime, but "for Libyans, and Libyans alone, there is the other way" (i.e., military action).

The Libyan military will almost certainly be the instrument by which Qadhafi is eventually removed. But present prospects for a successful coup attempt are slim. Moreover, because no widely acceptable alternate leaders have been identified, a military coup would most likely lead to further internal destabilization as disparate military commanders sought to assert a claim to power. Should this occur, continued evidence of the strength of regionalism makes it likely that Cyrenaican and Tripolitanian factions would once more, as in the past, find themselves at loggerheads over the nature and control of the political regime to be established.

Qadhafi's authority could eventually be eroded by competition between the military establishment and the young radicals—whose appetite for power has now been whetted. For the present, the radicals, who are motivated mainly by ambition and self-interest, appear well pleased with Qadhafi's leadership and the opportunities it affords them. But should the radicals eventually decide to unite against Qadhafi, they would portray him as a leader whose ideology has isolated Libya and whose domestic policies have alienated the Libyan people. Even then, however, a power play on the part of the radicals would depend on formation of an alliance with at least some military forces. Although a military commander might conceivably decide that alliance with the devil could be adjusted later, there seems little reason for military leadership to enter into a coup plot with radicals who have worked to dispossess the military of its position of power.

When Qadhafi's tenure does come to an end, his utopian and simplistic "Green Book" will certainly not survive him. However, the fact that Qadhafi has so radically changed the Libyan political order argues for the possibility that at least some vestiges of his philosophy—perhaps the revolutionary committee system—will continue, if only temporarily. What is more likely is that almost any Libyan successor regime will be less radical than the present one. However, given that Qadhafi's successor will almost certainly come from the military, with its heavy dependence on the Soviet Union, the next Libyan regime will still probably be left-leaning and anti-Western. As the Libyans maintain a fundamental distrust of the Soviet Union, however, some gradual movement toward nonalignment, as in the case of Algeria, could probably be expected.

QADHAFI IN PERSPECTIVE

The greatest damage done by Qadhafi has been that wrought against the Libyan people, who must endure his radical regime. Yet despite its excesses and radicalism, Qadhafi's rule has not been as bloody as that of many other dictators: Although several thousand Libyans are presently imprisoned on political grounds, relatively few have been executed. Equally obvious has been the national damage done to the Libyan economy and to the country's international standing. But beyond its borders, Libya under Qadhafi constitutes a strategic threat only to its immediate weak neighbors—Tunisia, Chad, Niger, and the Sudan—all of which are partially or wholly protected by Egyptian, Algerian, French, or U.S. defense arrangements. In the case of Chad, despite two invasions and years of occupation, Libyan forces have been unable to bring the entire country under their control.

Nonetheless, the image of Libya as an international threat has been stimulated not only by Qadhafi's support for terrorism but also by Western fears of a Libyan alliance with the Soviet Union and provision of a "forward base" to the Soviets for use of Libya's massive arms stockpile. But the Libyans remain extremely jealous of any Soviet military encroachments on their sovereignty, and much of Qadhafi's expensive military arsenal has, in any case, been rendered inoperative by improper storage. Isolation and fear of Western retaliation have pushed Qadhafi toward greater involvement with the Soviets, but his threats to join the Warsaw Pact if the West continues to pressure him are unrealistic. For their part, the Soviets are wary of too close a fellowship with Qadhafi and have not even signed the Soviet-Libyan Friendship and Cooperation Treaty agreed to in 1983.

Obviously, however, the world cannot ignore Qadhafi. He is certainly not likely to forsake the policies that have created such international consternation thus far. Although his tactics may be temporarily abated at times, he will not abandon his goals—for, in his view, the righteousness of his cause justifies whatever means are taken. It is also clear that Libya's access to such sophisticated weapons as the SA-5 missiles acquired from the Soviet Union in late 1985, as well as Libya's growing ties to proficient and determined international terrorist groups (in particular the Abu Nidal organization), render Libya a greater threat than ever to its neighbors and to European, U.S., and Israeli interests and facilities.

The correct way for democratic societies to handle Qadhafi without playing into his hands or stimulating him to greater extremism has not yet been identified. Severance of diplomatic ties by those states whose territory is the venue of Libyan terrorist attacks and an international boycott of Libya by international airlines would be appropriate. On a broader level, of course, it is clear that international cooperation, the strengthening of those countries most threatened by Qadhafi, and the appropriate levels of public condemnation, intelligence sharing, and cooperative pressure must be included among the strategies involved. Beyond such protective measures, however, there is little the international community can do short of outright hostilities.

It would appear, moreover, that public confrontation is counterproductive to international efforts to deter Libyan foreign policy excesses. Qadhafi thrives on public attention and benefits from the international lack of consensus as to how best to deal with him. Far from undermining Qadhafi, U.S. economic sanctions have provided a scapegoat to which he has pointed as the cause for Libya's difficulties. External threats, particularly threats of military attack, have the demonstrable effect of rallying Arab and Libyan public opinion behind Qadhafi and deflecting popular attention from the economic problems and political opposition that may eventually contribute to the overthrow of his regime. During the highly publicized Libyan-U.S. confrontations in August 1981 and early 1986, the Libyan military—instead of seizing the opportunity to topple Qadhafi—apparently set aside its internecine bickering in order to concentrate on national defense.

Public confrontation with Libya has also placed other Arabs, particularly moderate friends of the West such as Egypt and Jordan, in an untenable position. Qadhafi's ability to keep at the forefront of international opinion such themes as the Arab-

Israeli conflict and the Arab betrayal and exploitation by the
West has brought him considerable prestige among even those
Arabs who disagree with his ideology and actions. It is unrea-
sonable to expect any Arab government to risk siding with a
non-Arab force that places military or economic pressure on a
fellow Arab. Libya was unsuccessful in early 1986 in its attempts
to persuade the Arabs and the Organization of Islamic Conferences to adopt counter economic sanctions against the United
States. But the Arabs and Muslims did condemn U.S. threats
and military action against Libya.

The responsibility for dealing with Qadhafi remains with
the Libyan people. Until they remove him from leadership, they
and the rest of the world may simply have to cope. Qadhafi's
legacy to Libya may yet be the need for a massive effort at
national reconstruction, during which Libya will require all the
international support it can muster.

NOTES

1. Jacques Roumani, "From Republic to Jamahiriyya: Libya's
Search for Political Community," p. 168.

Chronology

1942	Qadhafi is born in Sirte.
December 24, 1951	Libya becomes an independent kingdom.
February 1953	Libya joins the Arab League.
December 1955	Libya joins the United Nations.
June 1959	Major petroleum deposits are confirmed at Zaltan in Cyrenaica.
1962	Libya joins OPEC.
September 1, 1969	Qadhafi comes to power in the "Al Fatah" Revolution
November 1969	Foreign banks are nationalized.
December 1969	First coup attempt made against Qadhafi.
January 1970	Tripoli Pact (union between Libya, Sudan, and Egypt) is announced.
May 15, 1970	Qadhafi calls for pan-Arabization of struggle against Israel through a pooling of all Arab resources.
June 1970	U.S. forces are evacuated from Libya.
September 28, 1970	Nasser dies.
April 1971	Federation of Arab Republics (Egypt, Syria, and Libya) is announced.
August 1971	Tobruk-Banghazi Declaration (proposed merger between Egypt and Libya) is agreed upon.

April 1973   Qadhafi issues his Third International
                 Theory and launches the Libyan "cultural
                 revolution."
July 1973   Unity march on Egypt begins.
September 1973   Foreign oil companies have 51 percent of
                 their assets nationalized.
October 1973   Third Arab-Israel war begins.
January 1974   Gerba Accord (union between Libya and
                 Tunisia) is announced.
April 1974   Qadhafi divests himself of all official titles in
                 order to devote himself to the formulation
                 of his revolutionary ideology.
May 1974   Jalloud visits Soviet Union and concludes the
                 first major Soviet-Libyan arms agreement.
1975   First imposition of U.S. economic sanctions
                 against Libya occurs when the United
                 States refuses to allow export of military
                 transport aircraft purchased by Libya.
August 1975   First significant coup attempt is made
                 against Qadhafi.
September 1975   Chad confirms Libyan annexation of Aozou
                 Strip held by Libya since 1973.
January 1976   First General People's Congress convenes,
                 and the Arab Socialist Union is disbanded.
January 1976   First serious antigovernment strikes and
                 demonstrations are held by university
                 students.
March 1977   Libya is established as a *Jamahiriyyah*, or
                 "state of the masses"; the Revolutionary
                 Command Council is abolished.
April 1977   Twenty-two officers implicated in the August
                 1975 coup attempt are executed (first
                 executions under Qadhafi regime).
July 1977   Egyptian-Libyan border war begins.
November 1977   Revolutionary committees are established.
1978   Government program to confiscate and
                 redistribute all land holdings of more than
                 24.7 acres (10 hectares) is accelerated.

March 1978	Announcement is made of real-estate regulations that virtually eliminate ownership of rental properties.
March 1978	Libyan cabinet is replaced by General People's Committees
May 1978	Libyan government issues new conscription law decreeing three to four years of military service for all Libyans between the ages of 18 and 35.
March 1979	Libya deploys troops to Uganda in support of Idi Amin against Tanzanian invasion.
September 1979	Libyan embassies become "people's bureaus."
1980	Compulsory recruitment of civil servants into the military begins.
March 1980	Private savings accounts are eliminated.
September 1980	Union of Libya and Syria is announced.
October 1980	Libyan regular army units are deployed into Chad.
Spring 1980– Fall 1981	First major campaign against "stray dogs" is initiated; eleven anti-Qadhafi dissidents are killed in Europe and the Middle East.
August 19, 1981	Two Libyan aircraft are shot down over the Gulf of Sidra by U.S. aircraft.
June 1983	Second major Libyan invasion of Chad begins.
Spring 1984	Assassination campaign against Libyan dissidents abroad is revived.
1984	State-run rationing system is set up to regulate supply of commodities and to combat black marketeering.
February 1984	Revolutionary committees announce that all Libyan exiles must return to Libya or face the "death penalty."
April 1984	British policewoman is killed by gunfire from Libyan people's bureau in London during anti-Qadhafi demonstration by Libyan exiles.

May 1984   Libyan National Salvation Front claims a
                 major coup attempt against Qadhafi.
July 1984   Treaty of Oujda (union between Libya and
                 Morocco) is announced.
July 1984   Libya is implicated in the mining of the Red
                 Sea and the Gulf of Suez.
September 1984   Apparent coup attempt at Misratah results
                 in the arrest of hundreds of military
                 personnel.
July–September, Sixty to seventy thousand guest workers are
  1985   expelled.
November 1985   Serious infighting in Qadhafi's inner circle is
                 reported.
January 1986   The United States accuses Libya of
                 complicity in late 1985 terrorist attacks at
                 Rome and Vienna airports; the United
                 States increases economic sanctions.
March 1986   U.S. air attacks are made against Libyan
                 patrol boats and the missile base at Sirte.
April 1986   U.S. air strikes are made against Tripoli and
                 Banghazi using F-111 warplanes based in
                 Great Britain as well as aircraft from the
                 Sixth Fleet in the Mediterranean;
                 Qadhafi's infant daughter is killed, and
                 two small sons are seriously injured.

Annotated Bibliography

Printed information about Libya remains limited by restrictions on researchers inside the country as well as by lack of interest outside. The following selected bibliography, intended as a guide to further study, contains most of the significant books on Libya published in English during recent years. Suggested reading on specific topics is included in the notes to Chapters 1 (history), 2 (society), 5 (foreign policy), and 6 (economy).

Internal events can best be followed by reference to the news media, in particular major newspapers such as the *Washington Post*, the *New York Times* and *The Times* (London), and to news and professional periodicals including *Africa Report*, *Les Annuaires d'Afrique du Norde*, *Magreb/Mashrik*, *Africa Confidential*, the *Economist*, and the *Middle East Journal*. The single most valuable source for current events in Libya is the Foreign Broadcast Information Service *Daily Report* (Middle East), which contains translations of Qadhafi's speeches and press releases from JANA, the official Libyan news agency.

BOOKS

Allan, J. A. *Libya: The Experience of Oil*. London: Croom Helm, 1981. Extremely well-documented discussion of the Libyan economy by a foremost authority.

———. *Libya Since Independence: Economic and Social Development*. London: Croom Helm, 1982. A companion volume emphasizing the impact of petroleum wealth on traditional society.

Anderson, Lisa. "Qaddafi's Islam." In *Voices of Resurgent Islam*, edited by John L. Esposito. New York: Oxford University Press, 1983. Concludes that Qadhafi, though devout and intent on using

Islam as a tool, is out of the mainstream of Islamic fundamentalism and will have no long-term impact on Islamic debate or reform.

Ansell, Meredith O., and al-Arif, Ibraham Massaud, eds. *The Libyan Revolution: A Source Book of Legal and Historical Documents.* Cambridge: Oleander Press, 1972. Contains basic documents of the revolution and immediate postrevolutionary period.

Cooley, John K. *Libyan Sandstorm: The Complete Account of Qaddafi's Revolution.* New York: Holt, Rinehart & Winston, 1982. Highly readable account of Qadhafi's rise to power and subsequent influence on Libya's internal politics and external relations.

Deeb, Marius K., and Deeb, Mary-Jane. *Libya Since the Revolution: Aspects of Social and Political Development.* New York: Praeger Publishers, 1982. A unique collection of essays dealing with topics such as the role of women and education under the "state of the masses"; based on research and personal observations in Libya during the late 1970s.

El-Fathaly, Omar I., and Palmer, Monte. *Political Development and Social Change in Libya.* Lexington, Mass.: D. C. Heath & Co., 1980. A pessimistic view of the potential of Qadhafi's revolution by co-author El-Fathaly, who served for several years as a government official under the Qadhafi regime. Heavy reading, but thought provoking.

El-Fathaly, Omar I.; Palmer, Monte; and Chackerian, Richard. *Political Development and Bureaucracy in Libya.* Lexington, Mass.: D. C. Heath & Co., 1977. Dated but valuable contribution to the small body of information available on internal Libyan developments.

Fergiani, Mohammed B. (compiler). *The Libyan Jamahiriya.* London: Darf Publishers, Ltd., 1983. Pro-Qadhafi survey of Libyan society and economic development.

First, Ruth. *Libya: The Elusive Revolution.* Middlesex, U.K.: Penguin Books, 1974. This classic study of the early postrevolution period was perhaps the first significant book to identify the destructive potential in Qadhafi's philosophy; essential and fascinating reading.

Habib, Henri. *Politics and Government of Revolutionary Libya.* Montreal: Le Cercle du Livre de France, 1975. A laudatory and biased—but instructive—account of reforms introduced or intended during the first five years of Qadhafi's tenure.

Hahn, Lorna. *Historical Dictionary of Libya.* African Historical Dictionaries, no. 33. Metuchen, N.J.: Scarecrow Press, 1981. Valuable collection of dates and terminology.

Haley, Edward P. *Qaddafi and the U.S. Since 1969.* New York: Praeger Publishers, 1984. Recounts the basic chronology of the devolution of U.S. policy toward Libya through 1982. Based on interviews with U.S. policymakers and other government officials.

Heikal, Mohamed. *The Road to Ramadan.* London: Collins, 1975. Deals only peripherally with Libya but provides a fascinating account of how the other Arabs, the Egyptians in particular, responded to Qadhafi's rise to power and why they were soon at variance with him.

Hinnebusch, Raymond A. "Libya: Personalistic Leadership of a Populist Revolution." In *Political Elites in Arab North Africa: Morocco, Algeria, Tunisia, Libya and Egypt,* edited by I. William Zartman et al. New York: Longman, 1982. Provides a description of the Libyan revolution as the crucible of a new elite; also describes Qadhafi's life experience—particularly his "intense personal identification with the 'Arab nation'" and his fear of alternate domestic power bases—as critical to present leadership dilemmas.

Joffe, E.G.H., and McLachlan, K. S. eds. *Social and Economic Development of Libya.* Cambridgeshire, England: Middle East and North Africa Studies Press, Ltd., 1982. Collection of essays of uneven quality, which, nonetheless, are useful to those seeking information about developments on such esoteric subjects as the evolution of music in modern Libyan society.

Khadduri, Majid. *Modern Libya: A Study in Political Development.* Baltimore: Johns Hopkins University Press, 1963. Detailed and readable account of modern Libyan history through the early years of the monarchy.

Lawless, Richard, and Findlay, Allan. *North Africa: Contemporary Politics and Economic Development.* London: Croom Helm, 1984. Useful examination of the interdependence of politics and economics in North Africa, including Libya.

Libya: A Country Study. Washington, D.C.: American University (Government Printing Office), 1979. Dated but still useful chapters on Libyan history, government, economy, society, and national security establishment.

Murabet, Mohammed. *Some Facts About Libya.* Malta: Progress Press, 1961. Prerevolution description of Libya, including still relevant data on geography and climate; out of print.

Neuberger, Benjamin. *Involvement, Invasion and Withdrawal: Qadhdhafi's Libya and Chad 1969–1981,* Occasional Paper No. 33. Tel Aviv: Shiloah Center for Middle Eastern and African Studies,

Tel Aviv University, May 1982. Provides information on the background and motivation for Qadhafi's first invasions of Chad.

Parker, Richard. *North Africa: Regional Tensions and Strategic Concerns.* New York: Praeger Publishers, 1984. Valuable discussion of Libya's regional context and relationships.

Reich, Bernard. "Socialist People's Libyan Arab Jamahiriya." In *The Government and Politics of the Middle East and North Africa,* edited by David E. Long and Bernard Reich. Boulder, Colo.: Westview Press, 1980. Provides a basic description of how Qadhafi came to power and what he hoped to achieve.

Villard, Henry Serrano. *Libya: The New Arab Kingdom of North Africa.* Ithaca, New York: Cornell University Press, 1956. Although rather pompously written, this brief account by the first U.S. ambassador to Libya contains interesting details on internal conditions at the time of independence.

von Grunebaum, G. E. *Islam: Essays in the Nature and Growth of a Cultural Tradition.* London: Routledge & Kegan Paul, 1969. Interpretive essays on Islam's growth and development by an eminent scholar.

Waddams, Frank C. *The Libyan Oil Industry.* Baltimore: Johns Hopkins University Press, 1980. A detailed explanation of postrevolution relations between the Libyan government and the petroleum-producing companies; traces the development of the Libyan oil industry and provides an overview of the economy.

Wright, John. *Libya.* New York: Praeger Publishers, 1969. A core book on Libyan history: well researched, detailed, and readable.

Wright, John. *Libya: A Modern History.* Baltimore: Johns Hopkins University Press, 1982. An articulate and valuable follow-on to Wright's earlier history in which the author balances political criticism with sympathy for the Libyan people.

Ziadeh, Nicola A. *Sanusiyah: A Study of a Revivalist Movement in Islam.* Leiden: E. J. Brill, 1968. Necessary reading for those seeking to understand the continuing power of religion and tribalism in Libya—and why Qadhafi has carefully sought to contain and control both.

ARTICLES AND PAMPHLETS

Alexander, Nathan. "The Foreign Policy of Libya," *Orbis* 24, no. 4 (Winter 1981).

Anderson, Lisa. "Don't Play Into Qaddafi's Hands," *New York Times* (September 18, 1984).
———. "Khadafy's Formula for Survival," *Boston Globe* (May 21, 1984).
———. "Qadhdhafi and the Kremlin," *Problems of Communism* (September-October 1985), pp. 29–44.
———. "Libya and American Foreign Policy," *Middle East Journal* 36, no. 4 (Autumn 1982), pp. 516–534.
"Background Notes: Libya." U.S. Department of State, Bureau of Public Affairs, April 1983 and August 1985.
Cooley, John K. "Pressures Mount on Libya's Qaddafi," *Christian Science Monitor* (September 26, 1985).
Damis, John. "Morocco, Libya and the Treaty of Union," *American-Arab Affairs*, no. 13 (Summer 1985), pp. 43–55.
Dobbs, Michael. "West Europeans Spurn U.S. Call for Sanctions Against Libya," *Washington Post* (January 4, 1986).
Dupres, Louis. "The Non-Arab Ethnic Groups of Libya," *Middle East Journal* 12 (1958), pp. 33–44.
Fallaci, Oriana. "The Iranians Are Our Brothers: An Interview with Colonel Muammar el-Qaddafi of Libya," *New York Times Magazine* (December 16, 1979).
Fialka, John. "Colonel Kadafi's U.S. Connection," *Washington Star* (four-part series, May 11–14, 1981).
"Focal Points," *Contemporary Mideast Backgrounders* (occasional series published by Media Analysis Center, Jerusalem).
"Focus on Libya" (occasional series published by Center for International Security, Washington, D.C.).
Henderson, George. "Redefining the Revolution," *Africa Report* 29, no. 6 (November-December 1984), pp. 36–42.
"The Libya Problem." U.S. Department of State, Washington, D.C. Bureau of Public Affairs, Special Report No. 111, October 1983.
"Libya Under Qadhafi: A Pattern of Aggression," U.S. Department of State *White Paper*, January 1986.
Mason, John P. "Qadhdhafi's 'Revolution' and Change in a Libyan Oasis Community," *Middle East Journal* 36, no. 3 (Summer 1982), pp. 319–335.
Murabet, Mohammed. "Tripolitania—The Country and Its People." Tripoli: U.S. Information Service, 1953.
Nasser, Omar. "Libya: Democracy of the Gallows," *Afrique-Asia* (November-December, 1984).
National Front for the Salvation of Libya *newsletter* (periodical published in Chicago, Illinois).

Novicki, Margaret A., interviewer, "Ali Treki: Foreign Minister, Socialist People's Libyan Arab Jamahiriya," *Africa Report* 29, no. 6 (November-December, 1984), pp. 19–25.

Ottaway, David B. "Grassroots are Choking Out Qaddafi's 'Direct Democracy,'" *Washington Post* (October 4, 1984).

Piper, Jessye. "Mu'ammar al-Qadhafi: Faces of 'the Enemy,'" *Co-Evolution Quarterly* (Spring 1984), pp. 44–52.

al-Qathafi, Muammar. "Green Book" (Part 1: The Solution of the Problem of Democracy—The Authority of the People; Part 2: The Solution of the Economic Problem; Part 3: The Social Basis of the Third Universal Theory). Tripoli, Libya: Public Establishment for Publishing, Advertising, and Distribution, n.d.

Ritchie, Michael. "Libya: Taking the Plunge with the GMR," *Middle East Economic Digest* (July 20, 1985), pp. 14–16.

Roumani, Jacques. "From Republic to Jamahiriya: Libya's Search for Political Community," *Middle East Journal* 37, no. 2 (Spring 1983), pp. 151–168.

————. "Libya: Exploring Terra Incognita," *Middle East Journal* 37, no. 1 (Winter 1983), pp. 89–93.

Seib, Gerald F. "Lower Oil Prices Put the Squeeze on Libya and Its Military Costs," *Wall Street Journal* (October 3, 1985).

Zartman, I. William, and A. G. Kluge. "The Sources and Goals of Qaddafi's Foreign Policy," *American-Arab Affairs*, no. 6 (Fall 1983), pp. 59–69.

Index

145

152 INDEX

officers, 73
reorganization, 73
salaries, 74
size of, 81(n4)
training, 67, 77
See also Free Unionist Officers
Military Intelligence Division, 85
Millet, 76
Milling, 115
Misratah, 6, 7, 29, 46
coup attempt (1984), 77
as province, 7
Mobutu Sese Seko, 90
Modernization, 29, 30, 35, 36, 37, 38, 39, 40–41
Mohammed (prophet), 31, 32, 45
Monarchy, 11–14
Montgomery, Bernard, 9
Moroccan residents in Libya, 98(table)
Morocco, 4, 21, 87, 92, 93, 104
Moro National Liberation Front (Philippines), 89–90, 104
Mubarak, Hosni, 92
Mukhtar, al-, Umar, 7
Municipal people's committees, 64, 65
Muqarief, al-, Muhammad, 79
Muslim Brotherhood, 76
Mussolini, Benito, 7

Nasser, Gamal Abdul, 13, 15, 43, 45, 48, 87
National Constituent Assembly, 11
National identity, 35, 36
Nationalism, 1, 8, 35, 129
Nationalization, 37, 77, 111, 112
National reconstruction, 134
Nation-state concept, 59
NATO. See North Atlantic Treaty Organization
Navy, 73
Neolithic hunters, 1
Netherlands, 114(table), 116
"New bourgeoisie," 40

New Caledonia, 103
New International Economic Order, 103
Newspapers, 17, 48
New Zealand, 103
Nicaragua, 103
Niger, 23, 28, 56, 91, 92, 94, 132
Niger River, 3
Nile Valley, 2
Nimeiri, Ja'afar, 79, 90, 94
Nomadic tribes, 2, 28, 30
Nonaligned Movement, 103, 132
North Atlantic Treaty Organization (NATO), 97
North Korea, 98
North Koreans in Libyan air force, 73
Nuclear research center (Tajura), 91
Nuclear technology, 91–92

Oases, 23, 24, 45
October War. See Arab-Israeli war, 1973
Oea, 2
Oil, 12, 115, 117, 122
boycott (1970s), 100, 112
companies, 111
discovery, 26, 108
exploration, 37, 117
facilities maintenance, 118
GDP share of, 108
grade, 111, 126
industry, 66, 74
market, 40, 107, 109, 127
production, 109, 111, 112
reserves, 108
wealth, 37, 107, 108, 110, 114, 125, 127
"weapon," 112
Olives, 24, 25
OPEC. See Organization of Petroleum Exporting Countries
Orchards, 75
Organization of African Unity, 103
Organization of Islamic Conferences, 134

DATE DUE